F

Also by John Gierach

The View from Rat Lake
Trout Bum
Fly-Fishing the High Country
Fly-Fishing Small Streams

A Fireside Book
Published by Simon & Schuster Inc.
New York   London   Toronto   Sydney   Tokyo   Singapore

Sex,
Death, and
Fly-fishing

John Gierach

SIMON AND SCHUSTER/FIRESIDE

Simon & Schuster Building
Rockefeller Center
1230 Avenue of the Americas
New York, New York 10020

Portions of this book have been previously published.

Designed by Diane Stevenson/Snap · Haus Graphics
Manufactured in the United States of America

10 9 8 7 6 5 4 3 2 1
10 9 8 7 6 5 4 3 2 1 PBK

Library of Congress Cataloging in Publication Data

Gierach, John
    Sex, death, and fly-fishing / John Gierach.
        p. cm.
    "A Fireside book."
    1. Fly-fishing. I. Title.
    SH456.G577 1990   90-32900
    799.1'1—dc20   CIP
    ISBN 0-671-70738-8
        0-671-68437-X PBK

CONTENTS

I stare into the deepest pool of the river which holds the mystery of a cellar to a child, and think of those two track roads that dwindle into nothing in the forest. I have this feeling of walking around for days with the wind knocked out of me.

—Jim Harrison

CHAPTER 1

SEX, DEATH, AND FLY-FISHING

On a stretch of one of the forks of a small river near where I live in northern Colorado, there is, in the month of July, a fabulous Red Quill spinner fall. As near as I can tell, it consists of at least three different species of these reddish-brown mayflies ranging in size from number 12s down to 16s or 18s. The fall lasts for weeks—sometimes more than a month—on and off, coming and going, overlapping, hardly ever the same twice.

No, I don't know which specific bugs are involved and, at the risk of insulting the entomologists, I'm not sure how much it would matter if I did. When the fall comes off, you fish one of the Red Quill or Rusty Spinner patterns in the appropriate size. When it doesn't come off, knowing the Latin name of the insect that is mysteriously absent lets you piss and moan in a dead language, but otherwise doesn't help much.

And there are plenty of evenings when this thing doesn't work out from a fishing standpoint, even though the bugs are at least in evidence on an almost nightly basis. As spinner falls go, this is the spookiest one I've seen, probably only because I've seen so much of it. Usually it has to do with the weather.

Here on the East Slope of the Rocky Mountains midsummer is the season for hot, clear, bluebird days punctuated by late afternoon thundershowers. Mayfly spinners—most of them, anyway—like to fall in the evenings when the light is low, and the air is cool and maybe a little damp. That's *a little* damp; a full-fledged rain can put them off, depending on the timing.

If the rain comes early enough in the day, it's over before the spinner fall should happen, and it has actually helped things along by chilling and humidifying the air a little. It's part of the local lore that an early shower can mean a good spinner fall later on.

If a thunderstorm comes late enough, after the flies have already formed up over the stream—and suddenly enough, without announcing itself with too much wind or cool air—it can flush the bugs into the water where the trout can get them.

This can make for some great fishing, provided the rain is heavy enough to knock the flies down, but not so heavy it makes the water too rough for the trout to see them—in which case the fish won't feed on them after all.

When that happens, you race downstream in your rain slicker to where the current pools out at the head of a small canyon reservoir in hopes that when the storm passes, the bugs will be collected down there and the trout will rise to them.

That's assuming the rain doesn't last too long, and doesn't muddy the water so much that the trout, once again, can't see the bugs on the surface of the stream, and, once again, won't eat them.

When the rain comes at its more normal time—a few hours before dusk, before the spinner fall should start—it may cool the air in the canyon *too much*, and cancel the event, although you might just hike up there anyway because some nights the weather clears off, warms up just enough (but not too much), gets very still, and the spinner fall is unusually heavy.

Sometimes.

Not always.

And I am not being sarcastic when I say that trout are known to be particularly fond of spinners.

On rare overcast, drizzly afternoons, the Red Quill dun hatch can last late, and the spinner fall can come early, giving you hours of good fishing with a transition point when both forms of the bug are on the water at once. Many trout can be caught on dry flies then if you're smart enough to notice what's happening with the weather, drop everything at home, and get up there early. Under gray skies and drizzle, dusk is usually too late.

Wet, gloomy summer days are unusual in semiarid Colorado, and this has only happened three times that I know of in something like ten years. I missed it once, although I sure heard about it later from some friends who were there. They caught lots of trout, including some big ones. It was great, they said, in a not so subtle tone of accusation.

The assumption out here is, you should always go fishing, period. If you don't, even for what might appear in other circles to be a good reason, the suspicion is that you are getting uppity or, even worse, lazy. You get some grief for staying home, and when the fishing was great, well . . .

People will forgive you for missing it once or twice, but no more than that.

On other days when I *was* there and ready, the air got too cool, or a stiff breeze came up, or the drizzle got too drizzly, or something. Once it was looking just right until a sheet of hail drew itself across the canyon like a gauze curtain, and my friend Koke Winter and I ended up huddling in the flimsy cover of a juniper tree getting whacked hard by a few less hailstones than if we'd been standing out in the open. A big one got me square on the back of the hand when I reached out to pick a nearly ripe raspberry. By morning I had a bruise the size of a quarter.

It was all over in about twenty minutes, and the evening slid into ideal, textbook conditions—cool, still, dusky, humid—except that not a single swallow flashed in the air over the stream to eat the bugs because there were no flies, and not a single trout rose for the same reason. The sky was clear with stars, the air was freshly washed and thick with clean, organic smells, the reservoir was a dark, disk-shaped mirror. To anyone but a fly-fisherman it would have seemed peaceful and quite pretty.

We figured the hail had killed all the flies and knocked all the trout senseless, so we went home. Koke doesn't drink anymore, so we couldn't even stop for a beer.

For the absolutely cosmic spinner fall, it seems as though perfect conditions have to also be *preceded* by perfect conditions, and I don't know how far back in time this meteorological juggling act has to go. I do know that even a slightly larger dose of what would normally be ideal is deadly. I suppose there's a lesson there.

It seems like your best bet for a workmanlike, day-to-day spinner fall is a clear, warm evening with no wind. This kind of conservative weather stops short of being the model of perfection, but it doesn't court disaster either.

The more you fish the more you start seeing these things the way a farmer does: it doesn't have to be great, just, please, don't let it be awful.

On those days you hike up the stream with the last direct rays of sunlight still on the water. This is a shallow, stooped-shouldered, forested canyon with a few rock outcrops at the water, and a few more standing up at the lip. The slope is gentle enough lower down to allow for some patches of wild grass. The stream has a sand and sandstone bottom, so even when it's clear it can seem to have a brownish cast to it. Some evenings it gets amber for a few seconds just before the light goes off it.

A good hundred yards downstream from the riffle we always start at, you can see the swarm of mayflies high in the air above the stream, dipping and climbing, their clear wings flashing. At these times they look like they're spinning, hence the name.

These particular mayflies seem to begin mating about the time the light goes off them. It's not a deep canyon, and it runs roughly east and west, so the sun stays on the water longer than you'd think it should. Not that you're likely to be impatient or anything. The bugs copulate on the wing, and then begin to fall on the water right around dark.

Sometimes, as the insects dip lower and lower over the stream, the odd, eager brown trout will jump out of the water and try to grab one. He seldom gets it. Nine times out of ten this is a little fish and you ignore it, but when it's a big trout you tie on an upright-winged Red Quill and cast it over there.

He almost never takes it. I know this to be true, but I have yet to figure out why. It should work but it doesn't, that's all.

Usually the few trout you see rising sporadically here and there while the spinners are still in the air will be taking ants, beetles, the occasional midge, errant mayfly dun, or caddis fly. Whatever happens to be around, in other words. This is not an especially rich stream, so the fish have learned to eat whatever is there.

On many nights the real spinner fall, and, therefore, the real hot fishing, begins after dark when you can't see what you're doing. You stumble over rocks, wade too deeply and ship water, snag your fly in the bushes, and tie wind knots in your leader that you don't know about until you hear them whistle past your ear. The question then is whether it will be easier to retie the leader or untie the knot, keeping in mind that you can't see what the hell you're doing in either case.

When you do get a good cast on the water, hints as to where your fly is and whether or not a trout has eaten it are sometimes telegraphed back to you in terms of spreading, starlit ripples and/or soft plopping sounds. But they're just hints. You can fish for hours without knowing for sure if you're using the wrong-sized fly, getting a bad drift, or if you're getting strikes you don't know about.

———

There are a few of us who fish this thing regularly, even though the trout aren't normally very big, and even though we often don't catch very many of them. The fact is, we seem to be truly fascinated by it, and I say that based on the evidence.

When we go up there and the spinners aren't happening for some reason, we don't tie on streamers or fish ants to the bank feeders because that might trash the water if the spinners actually do come on later. Nor do we work upstream to fish the pocket water with caddis flies because the spinners might come on while we're gone. We do a lot of standing around with spinner patterns already tied to 5 or 6x tippets, fly rods under our arms, hands in pockets, waiting. Sometimes there's a big beaver to watch, or little brown myotis bats to dodge. It can be nice and peaceful.

I like to think of this spinner fall as one of the great enigmas: the kind of thing that puts all the how-to-do-it fly-fishing writing in its place. If you hit it just right, the problem is not "How to Catch Trout During a Spinner Fall"—that's something you'll do without much trouble at all—but hitting it right is a matter of exquisite timing and some luck. It's the kind of puzzle where the challenge isn't to put the pieces together, but just to locate all the damned pieces in the first place.

We sometimes catch ourselves getting a little conceited as we stand out there in the dark without having landed so much as a single trout between us all evening. I mean, this is the really *difficult* fishing, definitely not for amateurs.

Someone finally says, "I'll tell ya, this isn't something for those guys who have to have 'big fish and lots of 'em,' is it?"

And someone else answers, trying to keep the uncertainty out of his voice, "Nope, it sure isn't."

For the moment at least, we fall into that class of fishermen who fancy themselves to be poet/philosophers, and from that vantage point we manage to pull off one of the neatest tricks in all of sport: the fewer fish we catch the more superior we feel.

———

Part of the fascination has to do with the mayflies themselves. We fly-fishers have a historic and abiding affection for them, and it's no wonder.

First there's that seemingly magical transformation. The insects spend most of their lives as downright unattractive bugs living under rocks on the stream bottom, but then, one day when all the signals are green, they swim to the surface to emerge as these really pretty flies. Even people who aren't especially interested in bugs will admit that mayflies are quite beautiful, at least after you've explained that they're not some kind of mosquito.

Beauty from ugliness, the sudden freedom of flight after a lifetime under a rock, and all that. It really is something.

These are the mayfly duns, and, as we all know, the ones that aren't eaten up by trout or birds fly to bankside bushes where they soon molt into spinners.

As pretty as the duns are, the spinners are even prettier. Their tails get longer and more graceful, their body colors brighten, and their wings get clear and sparkly. They're lovely, and this seems appropriate to us, because now the bugs' only chores in life are to mate and expire. Scientists call the whole group of mayflies Ephemeridae, from the same Latin that gave us "ephemeral," or "lasting for a brief time; short-lived; transitory." Even "tragic" if you want to stretch it.

We seem to have a real affection for the image of a beautiful insect that only lives for a single day (more or less) and whose only mission is to make love just once. They don't even eat. Poets got off on this as symbolic of the fleeting nature of life, love, and beauty until it became a cliché and had to be dropped or turned into a joke. The last literary reference I saw to it was in an old *Playboy* cartoon that showed a boy mayfly saying to a girl mayfly, "What do you mean, *'not tonight'*!?"

Mayflies and fly-fishing have always been inseparably connected (they're our favorite bug, after all), and that may be one reason why the sport is still seen as contemplative, even now with all our scientific and technical hoopla.

This really is kind of sweet, in a nineteenth-century sort of way, and it's not too difficult to attach religious overtones to it as well, but it's also efficient as all get out in a biological sense. Technically, this behavior is called semelparity, and it is de-scribed best by David Quammen in his wonderful book *Natural Acts:* "An animal or plant waits a very long time to breed only once, does so with suicidal strenuosity, and then promptly dies. The act of sexual procreation proves to be ecstatically fatal, fatally ecstatic. And the rest of us are left merely to say: Wow."

Quammen points out that bamboo trees (from which fly rods

are made) do it this way, and that salmon (on which fly rods are used) do it this way, too. I think that's interesting. Could there be some wild, metaphysical connection that makes fly-fishing incredibly sexy?

I sincerely hope so.

———

Mayflies mate and die en masse (it's been referred to as an orgy, but never as a mass suicide) probably at least partly for the same reason that large numbers of them hatch all at once: because hungry trout eat great numbers of them at these times and, with lots of the bugs making a break for it at once, some will get away to finish the business. It's a kind of suicidal diversionary tactic, and it works just fine in a system where the individual doesn't count for much.

The spinners mate and lay their eggs a little upstream from where the duns hatched, usually over a riffle, thus ensuring that the new eggs, as they wash downstream, will land on the bottom more or less in the same place the last batch did. If they hadn't always leapfrogged upstream like this; that is, if they'd mated and laid their eggs each season where they'd just hatched, they'd have slid downstream a few yards each year, and by now they'd have washed out to sea and become extinct.

And they don't all hatch or fall on the same day either. These things usually stretch over periods of days or weeks, and may start early one year and late the next as conditions dictate, so that something like a random storm or cold snap won't wipe out an entire population.

Hatches and spinner falls are large links in the general food chain, too. The bugs are regularly eaten by creatures like swallows, nighthawks, bats, and, of course, trout. Having the hatches and falls last for days or weeks ensures that the mayflies will survive into future generations, but it also means that trout and others can make dozens of meals out of them instead of just one.

Once the falls have started there are always a few stray,

expired spinners floating in shallow backwaters and stuck to weeds. These are clues. While waiting to see what's going to happen this evening, you can cruise the banks and at least see if there was a good rise the night before when you were somewhere else.

And nothing is wasted either. At the end of the spinner fall the few little dead bodies that aren't eaten by trout end up making a small but real contribution to the decomposing organic matter on the stream bottom that serves as fertilizer for more aquatic vegetation that is grazed upon by later generations of mayfly nymphs that hatch to feed new generations of birds, bats, fish, and so on.

It's nothing short of elegant, and the mayfly/trout connection we fly-fishers look so hard for is just a thin slice of it. There are also the game animals that drink from the stream, and the fishing birds that live on young trout, muskrats that eat the aquatic plants, and the swallows that eat the mayflies and live in the cliffs that were excavated by the stream itself.

A good ecologist can put dovetail into dovetail until the whole thing stretches out of sight. We call it an ecosystem now; earlier Americans called it the Sacred Circle. Either way it can make your poor little head swim with a vision of a thing of great size and strength that still depends on the underpinning of its smallest members.

It's a little harder to place our own role in all this because we're the ones doing the placing, so we naturally want to put ourselves at the top somehow, even though we don't actually fit there. Some say we humans have gotten to be so aberrant now that we don't fit *anywhere* in all this. I don't quite buy that, although it must be admitted that we're not exactly a harmonious species.

This fishing business probably has something to do with play—practicing a highly refined food-gathering technique as if it really mattered, even though we don't need the food and will probably release any trout we happen to catch. Play is what puppies do. It looks like good, innocent fun—and it is—but it also develops the predatory skills that will be needed later in life by the serious adult canine. Ever notice how *hard* a puppy can bite?

I don't know exactly what fly-fishing teaches us, but I think it's something we need to know.

———

A mayfly spinner lies on the surface of the stream in what fishermen call the "spent" position. To picture it accurately, remember that the insect has just had the first and only orgasm of its life and is now, in the natural course of things, dying from it. His body lies flush with the water, wings spread, legs out flat, tails splayed wistfully. Usually he's limp. If he struggles at all, he does it feebly at best. There's probably a silly look on his face, although it's hard to tell with insects.

Now picture seventy-five or a hundred of them lying on the water within casting range of where you're standing. As spinner falls go, this is not a terribly heavy one, though if you hit it right it's plenty heavy enough.

You have to imagine this even on-site because the bugs lying flat on the water are all but impossible to see. Even in good light their clear wings will have faded to nothing more than faint outlines, and the light will probably be turning a dull gray by now. It's very possible to fish a spinner fall successfully without ever getting a look at the bug you're imitating so carefully. It can become a matter of belief.

What you *will* see, if all is as it should be, are the distinctive rises of brown trout. The spinner rise is lazy, or at least businesslike, because, it's said, the fish "know" that the bugs are spent and won't get away.

There are differences of opinion about what trout know in an intellectual sense, but I have to buy the characterization. A trout feeding on an active insect—say, a mayfly dun, caddis fly, or even an egg-laying spinner fluttering on the surface—is likely to slash at it eagerly, but the same fish will sip the drifting spinners lazily. In slightly faster water, he might show the porpoising, head and tail rise, but that's about as excited as he gets.

This is important. How hard a trout works to get a given bite of food determines how many of those bites he has to take to first get even, and then make a profit, physiologically speaking. This goes right to survival, with no detours for fooling around or showing off.

During a spinner fall the fish will often ease down into the slower water below the riffle, or even to the tail of the pool. Why fight the heavier flows up ahead? The bugs have had it, and they'll be down here where it's easy soon enough.

Of course the trout understand what's going on. It's nothing less than conceited to think we do, but of course they don't.

———

The last time it all came together for me was two seasons ago. The weather seemed right, and my friend A. K. Best and I had driven past what was an almost sure caddis hatch on a nearby stream to check on the spinners. It was an act of bravado. It felt promising.

We saw the swallows weaving in the air first, and only spotted the bugs when we were at The Spot with the toes of our waders in the water. Even then they were just faint specks that showed up only because they were moving. There were no wings flashing in the last of the sunlight that evening. It was cloudy, cool for summer, threatening rain, but not raining yet.

We had the stream to ourselves because only tough, smart fishermen like us aren't afraid to get wet.

I don't know what A.K. fished with, although I'm sure he announced the pattern with the usual flourish. I tied on a #14 Michigan Chocolate spinner, a fly A.K. had turned me on to years before.

This thing has fine split tails of pale dun hackle fibers, spent hen hackle wings of the same color, and a thinly dubbed, dark brown body. Generally the feather wings of spinner flies are white because that's as close as most tiers feel they can come to clear with natural material, but A.K. had once told me that the pale dun wings become more realistically indistinct in the water

than the white ones everyone else uses. This from a man who
has been known to stop casting when the trout are biting, catch
a natural insect, and float it in a backwater next to his imitation,
cackling to himself if he likes what he sees, going silent and
thoughtful if he doesn't.

The flies began to fall, and the fish started to feed with just
enough light left to see by. It was all strangely matter-of-fact, as
things you wait for patiently sometimes are when they finally
happen. We picked what we thought were the biggest trout,
fished long, thin leaders to mimic the flaccid drift of the
spinners, and caught fish until past closing time at Andrea's
Cafe.

It was as simple as that.

———

The Red Quill spinner fall on the North Fork is one of the few
things in nature that I feel actually *belongs* to me and a few
friends. I don't mean it's a secret. In fact, during the weeks it's
on you'll see the odd new face from time to time. Often it's a guy
who's well-dressed, well-equipped, and who looks a bit out of
place, but he's sniffed this thing out and there he is, ready to
catch some trout.

He sometimes picks us out as locals (using the fly-fisherman's
innate skill for evaluating fashion and body language) and asks
us what the story is on this spinner fall he's heard about.

"Well, some nights it comes off and some nights it doesn't,"
we say. This sounds pointedly vague and useless and the guy's
brow furrows with suspicion. He's no kid. He's been snowed by
smart-assed locals before.

I guess we *are* exercising a little home-courtsmanship, but it's
basically the truth. That's all we really know about it.

Of course, waiting out there in the dark with the sky full of
bats and owls, we sometimes begin asking the great questions
that can kill time so nicely: sex, death, and fly-fishing; the
meanings of life and sport; are we real participants or just
observers, and what kind of difference does it make?

The new face, who may well disappear after a few more nights of this, joins in the conversation, but he remains wary and watchful. If something wonderful isn't about to happen, then why the hell are we all standing around like this?

CHAPTER 2

BASS FISHING by THE NUMBERS

I'm driving slowly and carefully down a dirt road that is uniformly pocked with hard-as-concrete, dried clay potholes. Assorted loose tools and cased fly rods can be heard shifting on the bed under the camper shell, but it doesn't sound as if any damage is being done. This is what rod cases are for, after all. The windows are down. The radio is off. A meadowlark is singing.

I'm taking it easy in the speed department because the pickup has been on way too many roads like this already and is the worse for it, and also because of my recent lunch: a Jumbo Double Chili Dog (microwave setting D) that I grabbed at the last minute on the way out here. It's appropriate that these things are sold at gas stations.

How is it that a back-to-nature-type, preservationist, catch-and-release fly-fisherman who admires all things plain and rustic feels free to eat cellophane-wrapped junk food for lunch five or six months out of every year? I guess it's one of the mysteries of nature.

I lurch down to the wide spot in the road on the eastern shore of Pond #1 and park the truck. It's a relief.

There are sixteen ponds here, scattered around in a large, rambling patch of western high plains wild grass and cottonwood country. This is a bright, open place with tall weeds by late June, usually too hot through the middle of summer days, but cool and green in the mornings and evenings.

Most of the trees stand in a grove along the creek that flows by a mile or more to the west. It looks inviting in there: thick, shady, with birdsongs echoing out of it, but you stay in the open because that's where the ponds are. The trees thin out as you go east, toward where the cars are parked. There's a lot of scrub, but also some enormous, ancient cottonwoods throwing wedges of shadow around them. A few are lying dead on the ground with exposed root balls the size of automobiles. Their trunks have stayed hard for years in the dry air.

These are bass and panfish ponds, although if you were a completely different kind of fisherman—one who used worms, or maybe a bow and arrow—you might think of them as good bullhead and carp water. Some do. A few of these things are nothing more than potholes, too small and shallow to hold anything but frogs and mosquito larvae, while others are big and fishy. It took me a decade of summers to decide which ones I liked best, and in that time some things changed, so I still lack a feeling of complete certainty about the place.

But then, certainty isn't exactly what a fisherman is after.

It doesn't seem to seriously bother anyone that the ponds themselves are numbered, but some of us have puzzled over why they're not numbered 1 through 16, as would seem logical, but rather 1 and 1-A through *15*. No doubt there's a person seated behind a desk somewhere who knows why that is.

———

A.K. is already here (typically early) and Jim Pruett (typically a little late) will come bouncing down the same road shortly—a little faster than I did, in a newer truck with fresher shocks. He'll have lunched on health food and mineral water. No preservatives, no cholesterol, no gas. This is a man who plans to live forever.

As soon as I step out of the cab A.K. walks over, flips open a plastic box, and shows me a handful of panfish poppers he tied up last night after a normal day—for him—of producing between ten and fourteen dozen flies for sale.

The poppers are, naturally, beautiful: perfect wispy tails of the best marabou, the tips of the fibers all even, but not clipped-looking; spun deer hair bodies packed tight as cork and razor-bladed to flawless symmetrical shapes. The colors of the tails and bodies match perfectly, of course. There are dark brown poppers and some bright yellow ones. Light and dark for the only two possible moods a sunfish could be in. Just something A.K. whipped up. They are so much better than what you actually need to catch a few bluegills that they're almost ostentatious, but this is, after all, what he does. So why not do it well?

I've known many a guide who, on his first day off in weeks, does not drive to the nearest town to drink, boogie, and/or meet ladies, but eagerly goes out fishing alone. It's different, and usually better, than baby-sitting a boatload of dudes. You can slow down, stretch out, do it right, see it for what it really is for a change. The same is true of fly tying. After whipping out many dozens of perfectly good flies for other people, you mix a stiff Canadian Club and water, and slowly, lovingly, tie a few for yourself. The fact that they're a lot better than they'd have to be to just catch fish is probably the whole point.

Once I've complimented A.K.'s bugs, we both begin to rig up. That means he only got here minutes ahead of me. Much longer than that, and I'd have found just his truck and a note. Once or twice when one of us was running late, we've fished together here without ever actually seeing each other. The place is just big enough for that to happen.

A.K. is just over a decade older than I am, but in recent years we have come to illustrate two distinct fly-fishing styles. He is in baggy, heavy, military-looking olive drab chest waders, while I'm struggling into a rust-colored, fashionably tight-fitting neoprene number that looks more like a wet suit. His hat is floppy, and is circled by a sheepskin band that holds at least a hundred flies, all used; my hat is an unadorned updowner. He'll be wading the shoreline making long, graceful casts, while I'm paddling around in a belly boat, or "personal flotation device," working a longer rod and a shorter line.

Rigging up is precise, but it's quick and nearly thoughtless. At the end of it we take large, gulping swigs of water from canteens—drinks big enough to last until after dark—and clean our sunglasses. Mine are aviator-style Polaroids strung around my neck on a cord. A.K.'s are prescription polarized bifocals.

True to form, A.K. has strung up a bamboo fly rod, but then so have I. For that matter, I also share some attitudes and other items of tackle with A.K. that could firmly place me in the last generation of fly-fishers, although that sort of thing isn't as obvious to the casual observer as how you dress. It just goes to show that stereotypes are seldom completely accurate. Still, someday we should have the series of pancake breakfasts it would take to raise the money for a bronze statue of A.K., complete with full-bent briar pipe. It would be a public service for the upcoming pastel fly vest and boron rod crowd. The brass plaque would read:

FLY-FISHERMAN—CIRCA 1950
LEST WE FORGET

Also true to form, A.K. will happily fish for bass today, and he'll do it well, but he will not go for more than a few days of it without reminding you that he considers them a cut or two below the mythical trouts. Given the choice, the fly-fisher with any breeding whatsoever always chooses the spotted, streamlined fish living in the colder water. Bass and the attendant panfish are amusing enough, but like triple X-rated movies and cheap wine, they are not something a gentleman spends a lot of time and energy on.

I, on the other hand, consider largemouths right up there with trout on the scale of respectability and have even been known to quote Russell Chatham to the effect that, if a bass and a trout of equal size were tied tail to tail, the bass would "tow that trout clear up to Healdsburg."

Panfish are just little bass that are easier to catch, and I like 'em a lot.

Furthermore, warm-water fly-fishing tends to be a long way from the poetic/ethical chess game of one-upmanship that trout fishing can become if you're not careful. It can be refreshing after too much "angling."

Granted, bass fishing in general is badly marred by its blood and guts, big-money tournaments and high-speed boats with electronic fish locating gizmos and jumpsuited drivers, but I'm talking about *fly-fishing* for bass on small ponds where your typical bass boat couldn't even turn around. Out here, even the most laconic, Latin-speaking fly-fishers seem to relax a little. Although fly-fishing for trout is now almost a science with these guys, the same method as applied to bass and panfish has remained, for reasons that are unclear, more of a folk art.

For one thing, either wading or flopping in and out of a belly boat, you get muddy out here, and your line picks up that green goo known as swamp snot and coats your line guides with it. The water itself is lukewarm to the touch and musky smelling, though it's cool enough that once you're in it the sweat dries stiffly in your shirt.

Ah, bass and bluegill fishing. There are days when catching trout from a cold, clear brook is just too clean.

It's a sign of our friendship that A.K. and I have, for many seasons now, taken this difference of opinion about bass and trout from the water, to the bar, and back home again without ever getting too hot about it. It probably has something to do with respect. In other words, I love the guy, even though he's wrong about bass—among other things.

And, just to set the record straight, I dearly love trout of all kinds, too, and actually spend most of my fishing time trying to locate and catch them. So much so, in fact, that one ex-wife was moved to say that I'd ruined my life over it, but wasn't going to ruin hers.

And I didn't either.

—

Just as we're ready to hit it, Jim arrives wearing a multicolored bicycle racer's cap in shades that probably wouldn't clash if your tastes were sophisticated enough. Just a few days before he had told me he was in the middle of a serious "hat crisis," but apparently he has decided to leave the fashion statement as it is for the moment. I have stashed the chili dog wrapper out of sight under the seat of my pickup so Jim won't see it. As he opens his car door I begin to fight the sudden urge to pass wind. I know Jim worries about how I eat, and, I suspect, about how I do a few other things, too. To his credit, he doesn't get motherly about it.

There are brief greetings. A.K. and I are ready, but not impatient. It's early, plenty of time. Still, Jim hurries to peel on his neoprene waders, string up his graphite rod, and shoulder his belly boat. Then we're off to look at Pond #5.

To the eternal credit of the agency that administers these waters, the ponds are not numbered on-site, although last season some signs connected with a nature walk program appeared explaining the presence of duck, goose, muskrat, beaver, and so on, giving some the impression that these creatures are here through the auspices of the Parks and Open Space Department. The pond numbers *are* on an official map that has been photocopied and circulated among some local fly-fishers. Only a few of the numbers have been replaced by names which, naturally, vary from one circle of anglers to another. Since descriptions and directions are cumbersome, the numbers have remained in wide use. I see this as a glitch in the overall aesthetics of the place, but a small and probably unavoidable one.

Collectively, these old abandoned gravel quarries have been a popular warm-water fishing spot for years. Once you could also hunt waterfowl here, but no more. Now it's a bird sanctuary, and also something of a bass sanctuary as well.

The size limit on largemouth bass is fifteen inches—a good bass on the western plains, though only pan-sized in the grand scheme of things—and bait fishing is now prohibited in all but the front two ponds: the ones you can drive right to and fish from lawn furniture within earshot of the car radio. It's been said they had to sacrifice these two ponds to the idiots to avoid too much squawking of the "I've been doing it like this all my life" variety, although the people in charge don't care to put it in quite those terms.

The new regulations, less than three seasons old at this writing, are designed to improve the fishing, and they'll probably do that if they're obeyed. Laurie Kuelthau, the local ranger (actually, they're called "wildlife managers" now) says the rules *are* being followed, and not just because of the more or less regular patrols either. It seems that most area fishermen, both fly and nonfly types, agree with the straightforward logic of special regulations: you can kill and eat little bass, or you can catch and release them until they get big, and it's a real choice. With the kind of concentrated fishing pressure a place like this gets, you can't have it both ways.

The few remaining meat hunters who sneak into the back ponds and fish bait can avoid the rangers, but not their fellow fishermen, from whom they're getting considerable grief these days. As Laurie said, "Peer pressure is the best enforcement tool we have."

In addition to the fifteen-inch limit, most of the ponds have also been stocked with grass carp.

"CARP!?" we all screamed.

Well, they're *sterile* grass carp—white amurs—that will supposedly not reproduce, but that will mow down some of the thick aquatic vegetation, allowing the bass to feed more easily on the abundant panfish. This should make the bass grow bigger faster as well as thin out the bluegill, pumpkinseed, rock bass, and crappie populations, which should, in turn, reduce the competition for food among those fish, and allow them to grow bigger, too. Coincidentally, a few less weeds should make the casting a bit easier, especially if you're working from shore.

It sounds perfect, and it could just be. Time will tell.

To a man, the fishermen I know will happily release bass

under fifteen inches, and most will do the same for those that push into the legal size: the ones that tape out at sixteen inches, seventeen, or twenty, or . . . Well, who knows? Some will do it thoughtlessly, exercising nothing more than an ingrained, day-to-day ethic, while others will do it out of simple curiosity, which is, after all, a large part of fishing. I mean, you can't help wondering just how big they *will* get. Already there are stories of a five- and a seven-pound bass. Even after you subtract the pound that was probably added by the fishermen who caught them, you're still looking at some nice fish.

———

Pond #5 is dimpled with the crisp, popping rises of panfish, but nothing that looks especially basslike. Then again, it's early in the day, a few hours yet from the time you picture in your mind when the late afternoon sun slants into early evening, the pond goes dark and glassy, and *the bass come out*. All the technical stuff notwithstanding, fly-fishing for largemouth bass is one part skill, one part fly selection, and eight parts timing, the bare fact of being there when it happens.

It's here that we split up. Jim will launch his float tube just around the bend in the Cattail Pond (#12), and A.K. will mosey over to the Cottonwood Pond (#13), which he's always had a thing for because it's easy to wade. I'll go in right here. The unspoken agreement is, if you're going to wait it out catching panfish, you might as well enjoy the luxury of having a whole pond to yourself.

Paddling the belly boat away from shore, I can hear and see yellow-headed blackbirds honking in the cattails where they've nested. A few weeks ago the red-winged blackbirds were in these spots, but the yellowheads move in a little later and invariably drive the smaller birds out of the prime areas. This is one of the signs you look for in the spring. The fish *may* be moving when the redwings are in, but the yellowheads mean they're on.

Some of the big Canada geese are still sitting on clutches of eggs on the ground (every year we find where coyotes or foxes have eaten both birds and eggs), but most are now towing broods of goslings around on the water. That's another sign.

Bluegills and pumpkinseeds come eagerly to the little yellow cork popper I've tied on, and I settle into the wonderful confidence of this kind of fishing. Whether or not you will catch panfish is seldom at issue, the only questions are "how many?" or "how big?"

Today it's "lots" and "not very." I work different kinds of water including a stony bar in hopes of some rock bass, try a different popper, and finally go underwater with a small streamer looking for the larger fish, but this time I don't locate them. I know where some coves littered with spawning beds are, but not in this pond. Today I'm prospecting, gathering information. Or, since I don't seem to care much one way or another and am doing all the right things by rote, maybe I'm just floating around in an inner tube on an early summer day pretending to be a fisherman.

The sun is bright, sky blue, air warm, water cool by comparison, and the belly boat—a clumsy load to haul in, even with the detachable backpack straps—is now like a mobile easy chair. I am overcome by a feeling of supreme self-indulgence, and can't for the moment, bring myself to worry about whether the bass will bite later or not, although this is a feeling I will get over soon enough. One of the most interesting elements of fishing is how the same things can matter so differently from moment to moment.

For instance, it begins to matter very deeply a few hours later when, also by unspoken agreement, we convene at the body of water known to us as the Bass Pond. This one is a longtime favorite of ours, and we tend to bristle some when we find other fishermen there, even though it's public and they have every right. Still, when you fish a place for enough seasons, you begin to feel proprietary about it.

This has always been a part of fishing, and it's an even larger part now that there are so many more of us. In a solitary sport, there's a very real sense in which your colleagues are also your worst enemies. In many places a kind of uneasy truce now exists and, although hostilities are seldom open, certain guerrilla tactics are sometimes employed. This is something you must live with, and even come to see the other side of.

No more than a week ago Jim and I, belly boats strapped to our backs, were heading for this same place when we met a kid with a spinning rod coming the other way. He asked if we were going to the Back Pond (another name for the Bass Pond—or #10) and we said yes.

"I just came from there," he said. "It's dead. Nothing happening at all. I think it's been fished out."

We thanked him for the tip.

Of course, the pond was boiling with fish, including some good-looking bass out along the weed beds that the kid couldn't have reached from shore, but that we could easily work from the tubes.

I remember thinking, Nice try, kid. A little clumsy and obvious, but still a nice try. If we'd been new around here, or stupid, it might even have worked.

What I should have said to him is, "Look, there's an art to this. Next time, don't volunteer so much so soon. It makes people suspicious."

We older bullshitters really should help the young ones who are just coming along.

The pond is not exactly boiling this evening, but it's beginning to simmer nicely, even with some sunlight still in the air. Against a backdrop of sporadic sunfish rises, the odd bass swirls ominously. Is it a single fish cruising, or several, each one wallowing in his own spot? You can't tell. And it doesn't matter. By the time you figure it out—if you figure it out at all—it will have changed.

A.K. walks down to a weedy cove and begins to cast one of his bright yellow Spruce Fly streamers. This is a color variation on the old standard pattern. It's good for brown trout and, coincidentally, for bass. A.K. *does* own some real bass patterns, but would just as soon not get too involved with a warm-water-fly selection.

Jim and I tie on cork-bodied poppers and launch the float tubes.

There is drama in the air, but the air itself is deeply quiet. A car passing on the paved county road a half mile away whooshes at about the same volume as the fly lines in the air. It's past suppertime, so the rumbling machines and backup beepers at the ongoing sand and gravel operation on the west bank are mercifully silent.

The mildly industrial feel of this pond turns some people off, but I sort of like it. For one thing, it serves as a kind of camouflage, keeping those people away who are stuck on a postcard image of fishing, even for bass. For another, I like being reminded that as the gravel company meandered across this piece of land, it left behind it holes in the ground that naturally filled with groundwater, and, in time, turned wild. Just as naturally, some people put fish here, and then, later, other people came to catch them out. This is the kind of long-term industrial pollution I can live with.

The ponds have to be managed now because eventually too many of us came, and in roughly two decades I've seen the place change from one where people could take a few fish to eat into one where different people with better tackle come to perform Sport. It's a change for the better, given the realities, but I now and then miss talking to the businesslike, straw-hatted fish killers who reminded me of my childhood. These were guys with perspective, and the patience to watch a bobber; people who fished ten-dollar glass rods and who dug their own bait because then the fish were virtually free. I don't know where they went. They're illegal out here now, and all but extinct.

Meanwhile, nine to five, the gravel company digs the holes that could one day become ponds #s 17, 18, and 19, or, more likely, 16-A, -B, and -C.

CHAPTER 3

Midge Fishing

Once upon a time, early one morning in the lobby of a small resort lodge, a flytier was sitting at a table cranking out #26 midge flies. He was intent, both because of the small size of the hooks he was working with and because he seemed to be in a hurry. Fishermen tying flies on-site are almost always in a hurry.

The man's expression seemed to combine hope, the usual hint of doubt being overcome by conviction, and, of course, impatience. This was clearly the fly that worked yesterday and that he'd run out of, or the one that *would* have worked yesterday if he'd had it. This pattern was going to produce, if only through the sheer effort of will. You could see that in the guy's eyes. At his elbow was half a cup of coffee that looked cold, with the nondairy creamer beginning to form a scum.

It was about then that a well-dressed woman—the kind that is sometimes referred to in places like this as a "tourist lady"—detached herself from her entourage and breezed over with scarves flying and bracelets jangling. She squinted theatrically at the tiny fly in the vise and shrieked, "Goodness! What kind of silly little fish do you catch with *those*!?"

(For the uninitiated, the shank of a standard size 26 hook is about three-sixteenths of an inch long.)

Without stopping or even looking up, the flytier replied, "Silly little trout, madam."

A good answer, I thought: brief, somewhat accurate, a little sarcastic, not really hostile, but leaving no room for further discussion. There are mornings when a guy really doesn't have time to chat.

Of course, you can't blame the lady either. In nonangling circles fly-fishermen are often viewed as being pretty extreme, and when you see one tying flies so small it would take half a dozen or more to cover a dime it can start to look downright compulsive. I guess you have to remember that those who don't fish often see those of us who do as harmlessly strange and sort of amusing. When you think about it, that might be a fair assessment.

————

When I started fishing for trout with a fly rod, midge fishing was already in place as one of the sport's newest, grooviest developments, so I naturally took it up. It had surfaced in a big way in the early sixties when the tiny hooks (down to size 28) and the very fine leaders to tie them to arrived on the fly-fishing scene. Before that, the entomology was generally available, but the technology wasn't, and about the smallest hook you could get was a size 20. At least that's the smallest hook any fishing writer ever talked about, usually adding an exclamation mark to make the point. These suckers are *really little*, folks!

You could make a case that the appearance of hooks sized into the 20s was the last genuinely new wrinkle in the sport of fly-fishing. I mean, other developments have helped us to do the old things faster, easier, and maybe even a little better, but the miniature hooks and leaders allowed us to imitate bugs that we just *could not* copy before—the hatches that had previously left even the best fishermen sitting on the bank bitching among themselves while the trout rose happily with no one to bother them.

It was new ground.

Not only that, it was seen as a class act—the ultimate in delicacy in an already delicate sport—and it was difficult, too. It *had* to be difficult, right? The flies were minute and they were tied to leaders that were, as every fishing writer worthy of the name pointed out, "cobweb fine." This was sublime stuff to the guys who liked to have the odds against them.

For a while the term "midge fishing" was commonly used to mean fishing with any fly size 20 or smaller, regardless of what it was tied to imitate. The idea was to catch the largest fish possible on the smallest flies imaginable so that the whole thing would be improbably heroic—like bagging a rhino with a .22, only safer.

Arnold Gingrich even invented the 20/20 club: all you had to do to become a member was land a twenty-inch trout on a size 20 fly. At the time, that was about the toughest—and therefore the classiest—thing you could do with a fly rod in fresh water.

Incidentally, I just heard about the modern version of the 20/20 club. This one involves landing twenty fish in a single day that are all twenty inches or over. Fly size is not considered. I like the old one better. Gingrich was a gentleman sportsman whose attention span was such that he could appreciate the single trout caught well. This new thing strikes me as the catch-and-release equivalent of those old, brown photos showing two guys in derby hats grinning over 173 dead fish.

The new-age fly-fishing consciousness has not, apparently, entirely done away with that kind of egotistical greed.

———

So, for a while any small fly was a midge, but pretty soon the sport's tendency toward entomological accuracy began to take over. The bug men knew that a midge was, properly, one of the little two-winged, nonbiting aquatic flies of the order Diptera, so "midge" came to mean just that, while the other tiny bugs these guys were imitating (the mayflies, ants, jassids, and such) were lumped under the heading of "minutiae." I clearly remember stumbling onto that distinction early on because it gave me a real sense of what I'd gotten myself into. There was some concentrated nit-picking going on here and you were expected to know your stuff.

If you wanted to call yourself a midge fisherman in the 1960s, it was expected, in certain circles at least, that you would not only know your stuff, but also buy into the rest of the program, which included a short, very light rod (preferably split bamboo), a pocket-watch-sized reel (preferably English), and an overall tendency toward the esoteric (preferably expressed in Latin).

Some extremes were reached.

Any short, light rod was suddenly a "midge rod," and some makers, honestly curious about how far their craftsmanship could reach in this direction, stepped over the thin line that separates a workable piece of fishing tackle from an expensive gimmick.

Some beautiful rods were produced: lovely doll-like things weighing only a few ounces, with hand-planed, six-strip bamboo tips thinner than matchsticks. There was no choice but to be impressed, even though many of these things seemed more like scale models of fly rods than the real articles.

I'd been fishing more or less successfully with little flies for some time, but when I reached that inevitable point where my midge fishing fantasies had to be propped up by something extravagant, I went out and bought a darling little seven-foot Leonard bamboo that a friend was unloading because he was strapped for money. This wasn't the shortest or lightest rod you could find, but it was still a midge rod in the finest sense, that is, it was real pretty, beautifully made, and nicely balanced, but it was too noodly for even the lightest line then available, which was a 3-weight. It also lacked guts, or authority, or whatever you call the attribute a fly rod possesses that lets you cast where you want to and play fish convincingly.

I was a little disappointed, but I got over it.

I almost kept the rod anyway, as a collector's item, but finally turned it over on the premise that you shouldn't have too many things around the house that you never use. By then the place was starting to look like a sporting goods museum anyway. Not,

unfortunately, the Museum of American Fly Fishing; more like
one of those roadside SEE THE TWO-HEADED RATTLESNAKE joints.

———

Another extreme was the eyeless size 32 hook, although few,
including perhaps even the manufacturers, took this one very
seriously. If I remember it right, one of the ads said something
like, "Try tying a Royal Wulff on one of these!" Which,
naturally, some did.

It's entirely possible that more size 32 flies were exhibited in
tackle shops to illustrate the skills of some local tier than were
actually fished. Maybe the practical limit on size was exceeded
with a hook too small to have an eye. If you wanted to actually
fish with one of these things, you had to tie the fly with a snell
of 8x monofilament, which appeared on the market at about the
same time.

A full box of size 32s spilled on a table looks like a small pile
of bronze-colored sawdust.

———

When it comes to miniature flies there are three kinds of
fishermen: those who shy away from fishing midges entirely,
thinking it's too difficult for them (they're probably wrong) or
that it approaches being ridiculous (in which case they may be
right). There are others who fish them when they have to in
order to catch trout, and still others who would rather fish to a
midge hatch than anything else. And the smaller the bugs the
better they like it.

Among this last group are the people who are buying the new
2-weight rods that are on the market now, and the craziest of
those will retire the 2-weights and run out to buy the even newer
1-weight. Whether or not this thing is a real fly rod remains to be
seen, but it may turn out to be the last word on the subject, a
hard act to follow.

Extremes.

—

I didn't buy out of midge fishing when I sold that little seven-foot Leonard, I just realized, along with a lot of other fishermen, that you don't need a miniature rod to fish miniature flies. In fact, something like an eight-foot, 5-weight is much better. A rod like that gives you more distance, more punch in the wind, and more choices. In other words, what do you do if you're out fishing midges with your 1-weight and decide that the answer is actually a weighted size 2 stone-fly nymph or a stretch-bodied, full-dressed streamer? And what do you do when the wind blows?

It's possible to specialize yourself right into a corner, not only with a rod that's too light for normal fishing, but with the tantalizing idea that you're somehow superior to everyone else because you can see well enough to tie a #24 fly to a 7x tippet. The sport of fly-fishing tends to breed these kinds of attitudes, but, to its credit, it also tends to drop them after a while. Many of us still fish with the tiniest of flies, and we enjoy it, but it's rare now to see someone puff himself up like a tomcat and call himself a Midge Fisherman.

For that matter, you don't even need a fly rod. There are a lot of fly-and-bubble spin fishermen here in Colorado who do very well on the mountain lakes using midge flies on ultralight rods, two-pound lines, and the smallest casting bubbles they can find. These guys sometimes refer to the insects in question as "punkies" or "snow flies," catch lots of big trout, and otherwise aggravate that peculiar breed of fly-fishermen who think of themselves as operating in the rarefied atmosphere of high sport where certain people shouldn't be allowed to intrude.

Speaking of mountain lakes, this is one kind of trout fishing where midge flies are a must. Regardless of what other food forms live in a high lake, it's the staple midges that can hatch on any day when the water isn't frozen, and probably will.

I think still-water midging is the hardest fishing I've ever done, and I don't say that just because I recently spent a fishless day on a lake in the Indian Peak Wilderness, although that does bring it all vividly to mind.

The day is chilly, still, and overcast; not exactly threatening rain—or possibly snow—but definitely considering it. Cosmic midge weather. The surface of the lake is smooth and dead calm except for the random, dimpling rises of a few cutthroat trout.

The midges are hatching lazily and the fish cruise either aimlessly or in complex patterns known only to themselves. You know that if there were more bugs you could get gulpers—trout rising often enough and in a tight enough rhythm that you could determine their direction and lead them with your cast. But there *aren't* more bugs. It's the reality of the sport: there are only as many bugs as there are, period. Take it from there.

There are at least two different flies on the water, a #26 cream and a larger, #22 black. The trout will probably take either, but you tie on the #22 because it's bigger—if you can use the word "big" properly in this context. You cast it out there and watch it.

And watch it.

There are rises in the neighborhood, but you have no way of knowing if fish are seeing your fly and rejecting it or not seeing it at all. Figuring the odds of a random trout swimming under a random midge fly on the surface of a fifty-acre lake in a period of an hour is the kind of thing that would take some serious arithmetic to figure out, and my belly boat, not being an executive model, is not equipped with a calculator.

After what seems like a very long time, you reel in and switch to a subsurface pupa pattern. This you retrieve slowly, hoping the movement will attract some attention. If nothing else, it will cover a bit more water, though possibly not enough to make a difference. It will also give you a little something to do.

You could have done this with the dry fly—the spin fishermen do it all the time—but you're a *fly-fisherman* and therefore a fanatic for accuracy. To adjust the action you need a different fly, never mind that your fingers are now too cold and numb to tie a good knot.

About then you hear a tremendous *sploosh* as a large trout leaps from the water in a rise form as uncharacteristic of a midge-eating fish as you can get. You wonder about that until, a few moments later, a caddis fly the size of a small butterfly blunders past as an explanation. You fight the obvious temptation to tie on a big caddis pattern, noting pointedly to yourself that this was one rise out of hundreds and that every other fish in the lake is calmly sipping midges.

You begin to pine for a stream where the fish stay in one place; where you can show them a fly and figure they've probably seen it; where you can then change patterns if the first one doesn't work and otherwise fall into the usual trout technician mode. It occurs to you that a small stream flows into this lake at the west end and back out to the east. You know you could catch a trout or two at either place, but you also know that at this time of year the real torpedoes live in the body of the lake.

This is the inevitable moment of indecision, when the mind begins to wander. You begin to realize that you're feeling the effects of belly boating for a long time in a very cold lake. For instance, you can't exactly locate your legs.

And so it goes. It's possible to catch no fish in a situation like this, and the #22 fly and 7x tippet do make it seem like incredibly difficult fishing. On the other hand, not catching trout on midges is no harder than not catching them on size 2 streamers.

———

The first midge dry flies I saw for sale were nothing more than bodies and sparse hackles on little bitty hooks. Nice and simple. I copied some at my own vise, they worked, and similar flies work to this day, but by now the great minds of flytying have applied themselves to midges, and there are dozens of neat and effective patterns around.

Midge flies have wings now because the real insects have wings, never mind how hard they are to tie or whether or not they make any difference to the trout. That's the kind of logic that has overtaken fly-fishing and I, naturally, buy it as much as the next guy.

The wings on my midge dry flies are made of feather—mallard duck or pheasant primaries, depending on the desired color—while the ones on A.K.'s patterns are now usually made from a thin strip of a kind of waffle-patterned plastic. His are more durable and slightly easier to see on the water, mine are more organic. This may reflect two philosophies of flytying or may just be because I used to be a hippie and A.K. used to be a dance band saxophone player. Both styles of fly have been known to catch fish.

We both tie these in sizes 18 all the way down to 26 and occasionally even 28. No 32s.

My favorite subsurface pattern is the String Thing. It imitates the little midge larvae, those tiny, bottom-dwelling, wormlike things that look like pieces of thread. In good midge streams you fish them right on the bottom, with a dead drift, when nothing more interesting is happening. You don't usually hammer fish this way, but you'll often pick up a few when you might well have gotten skunked otherwise.

A String Thing is nothing more than tying thread wrapped onto a bare hook to form a thin body, and even then it's too fat to exactly imitate the actual creature in question. Some tiers have tried to add darker heads or nearly invisible wisps of something for legs, only to find that they've screwed it up. In fact, if flytying hooks came in the right colors—rust, tan, olive, and cream—then a small bare hook would be the perfect copy of a midge larva.

Although any professional flytier would be happy to make String Things commercially, they just don't sell. The problem is, when they're offered in a fly shop (at any price), even customers who don't tie their own flies look at them and say, "Shoot, I can do that myself." And they can, too.

In a way the String Thing violates something essential in the aesthetics of flytying by being so idiotically simple to tie. On the other hand, it's right in the mainstream by being an almost exact copy of the bug in question. It has been known to freak people out, and even for those of us who like it, catching a fish on one can be an exercise in mixed emotions.

When it comes time to hatch, the larva turns into a pupa and swims for the surface where it emerges into the winged adult. Trout eat a lot of them then, and a pupa pattern is a good one to fish in the earlier stages of a hatch when there are lots of these things cluttering the water.

I think the best pupa patterns are the simplest: a thin body of some kind with a sparse shoulder of dubbing. Materials are a matter of personal preference. Some like dubbing, others swear by stripped quill, although this can be fragile. Then again, what isn't fragile in near microscopic amounts? The fact is, if you get into fish you're going to tear up midge flies, but then you're catching trout, so you're not supposed to care.

Whatever you do, don't get too fancy with these things. A midge pupa in the water looks about as complicated as a comma on a printed page.

Midge emergers can be really effective patterns and I think the best are the ones with something tied off the back of the hook to give the impression of the trailing pupal husk in that transitional instant in every midge's life when he's a winged fly with his butt still stuck in the empty shell of what used to be the pupa.

Sometimes the wings on the fly are folded or rolled, and sometimes they're all the way out. The trailing shuck can be mallard flank, a whole small hackle feather, plastic, marabou, ostrich herl, you name it. Flytiers will try anything once and there's seldom just a single answer. The size of these insects is somehow reflected by the infinitesimal snippets of material that can make all the difference to the fish.

In a way flytying is like the best photography: it doesn't so much copy something as it freezes an instant in time. Ken Iwamasa, who puts in a lot of hours studying and photographing such things, says that it usually takes only three or four seconds for a midge to free itself from the pupal shuck, thus changing from what we'd call an emerger to what we'd call a winged dry fly. A couple of seconds—but there are times when the trout only want to eat those bugs that are caught briefly in that

awkward position. And when that's what the~~y~~
by God, is what you'd better give them.

This part of it isn't a matter of going to ext
of making a fine and meaningful distinction. This p
distinction has to do with moments that can be dealt with
profitably or otherwise—or that can just be watched as they pass
by—but that do, nonetheless, pass on by. This idea of seizing
the instant is what keeps fly-fishing a sport in the face of all our
efforts to make it into an art.

One thing you can do that I think is very neat is tie in your
trailing husk material at the middle of the hook shank and then
tie a small body and wing ahead of that. What you get here is a
nice-looking emerger, but, more than that, you can get, say, a
size 24 fly on a #18 hook. When you're working this small, any
help you can get in the hooking department is a real advantage,
and there's also a kind of sly satisfaction to be gained by playing
two tricks on the same trout at the same time.

All fishing has to do with playing tricks, and the neater the
illusion the greater the satisfaction. Midge flies are hard to
make, frustrating to handle, difficult to tie onto fine tippets in
low light with numb fingers, and not all that easy to hook fish on.
Consequently, they're great fun.

Midges also let you stretch out into odd corners of the year
when the bigger, easier hatches are off; when, without these
ridiculous little bugs, the trout would go hungry and the
fishermen would be hunting ducks or sitting home drinking.
Midge hatches are most "important," as they say, early and late
(like in March and November) when catching trout on dry flies
seems even more unlikely than it usually does.

These are the times when you can get pretty intense, when,
in fact, you *have* to be intense to get into the proper spirit of the
thing.

It was in February of last year when I came upon A.K. sitting
on a rock next to the South Platte River. It was a cold, bright
day. A few trout were rising sporadically in dead smooth,
painfully clear water. As far as I could tell—and I'd tried hard to
tell over the last few hours—there was nothing whatsoever on

the water for them to feed on. I had been reduced to wandering up and down the stream trying not to wish I was back home doing something constructive.

When I found A.K. he was sitting on a rock at the side of a long, smooth glide that was just barely braided at its upstream end by a slow, narrow tongue of current. There were three trout dimpling the surface out there, on the far side of the crease, and one of them looked pretty good. I'd left A.K. at this very spot two hours ago. He hadn't moved ten feet in that time, and now he was busy clipping the hackles off a size 28 winged dry fly because, he said, he thought it was "too bushy."

Here was a man at the absolute edge of impossibility with a pair of scissors in his hand and a slightly mad look in his eye, and I told him so. I've always tried to stand up for the traditional aspects of the sport, and one of the things midge fishing has cost us is that poignant moment when the water is too low, the flies are too small, and you just can't go on any longer: the moment when a guy is required to lean his rod against a tree, turn to his partner, and say, "Well, shit." Then you find a roadhouse, get sloshed, and plan another trip.

That's how it's supposed to work.

But then A.K. waded in at the head of the glide, made a long, downstream pile cast, and hooked a trout. It was the big one, of course, the one in front. My rod was leaning against a tree, and I kicked it over on my way down to the water to watch him land his fish.

CHAPTER 4

EXPERTIZING

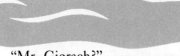 The guy called me from his office, or, rather, his secretary called.

"Mr. Gierach?"

"Speaking."

"Please hold for Mr. So-and-So."

And there I was—eight in the morning, conscious, but only halfway through my second cup of coffee, listening to a soulless elevator arrangement of a Beatles tune. And I hadn't recognized the name either. I considered hanging up, but I was curious. If this turns out to be a salesman, I thought, I'm gonna say something really unpleasant about his mother.

But no, when the guy finally came on the line he turned out to be someone who'd read my stories and liked them—clearly a man of taste and breeding, even if his telephone manners weren't great. He told me that he had recently moved to an exclusive, private subdivision that had an equally private trout lake on the property. Very posh, very costly. The lake was filled with huge rainbows, but it had turned out to be a tough, moody body of water, and in the six weeks he'd lived there he hadn't been able to catch any fish. Not one. He found this situation to be unacceptable.

"I'd like to have an expert show me how to get them," he

said. It took me a few seconds to realize he wasn't asking me to refer him to an expert: he meant me.

The man didn't exactly sound desperate, but there was a grave edge to his voice as he said that *others* had caught big rainbows from the lake that very summer. Some of the fish had been as heavy as nine pounds. I didn't bother asking him if he'd seen the fish or if the person or persons who caught them would be likely to lie about something like the weight of a large trout. It didn't matter. Nine pounds or only seven and a half, I grasped the problem.

You know how you get a vision of someone over the phone by listening to the voice while staring out the window at a familiar cottonwood tree? I saw the guy as clean-cut, late thirties, with a six-figure income, large wardrobe, and a no-nonsense attitude. It was just a guess, but I also thought he might be someone who had negotiated one of those arrangements—spoken or other-wise—that fishermen sometimes make with their nonangling wives: we live in the country, but not too far from town; you get the big house with the stained glass, I get the private lake (and maybe a new canoe), and we live happily ever after, okay?

I've seen this attempted before. It takes some money and a little slack on both sides, but it has been known to work.

And now there the guy was, six weeks and no fish, and he was calling me. I figured that with a little luck I could save the marriage. Getting on this private lake with all the huge trout in it was a secondary consideration.

So I rose to the occasion, as they say, and suggested that I bring along my friend A.K., whom I accurately (and carefully) represented as "at least the expert I am."

"That'd be just fine," the guy said.

I already knew where the lake was, as do most of us locals. It's behind a formidable-looking fence, on a chunk of real estate between here and town where widely spaced, rambling homes hide modestly behind elaborate but tasteful landscaping and lots of trees. All you can see of the lake from the road is the earthen dike on its east end.

It looks quiet and ordered back in there, and I'm sure one of the selling points has to do with security. Residents get in by punching up a personal code that automatically opens the wrought-iron gate. Guests call the house they're visiting and are buzzed in. Everyone else stays the hell out.

I've never actually been offended by this approach to life—privacy is a valuable commodity, after all—but I'd always gotten a slight James Bond rush when I drove by the place: the feeling that getting into the compound would take either some nicely forged papers or a black sweater and wire cutters, but it would be possible. I'd never tried it either way, but, to be honest, it had crossed my mind. I guess I fished for too long as a kid to ever completely outgrow that sense of challenge that's presented by a fence. And the sturdier the fence, the more it gets you to thinking.

The word around was that the lake was pretty good, but then that's always the word on lakes behind tall fences that no one you know has ever fished.

A.K. and I showed up at the appointed time with the full arsenal loaded in a pickup truck: several fly rods each, light to heavy; a selection of lines, floating to full sinking; all the flies either of us could dig up, which was a lot; plus waders and float tubes. In other words, we were in full fly-fishing SWAT team mode. The iron gate slid aside for us, and a woman who was on her way out gave us a rather cool glance, probably figuring we were there to clean someone's septic tank.

Our host (a clean-cut man in his late thirties) met us at the lake. He had a brand-new Old Town canoe lashed to the roof of his Saab. After the introductions, A.K. and I began to rig up while our host sat down in the shade of a box elder tree and cracked a can of imported beer.

"You're not gonna fish?" A.K. asked.

"Not just yet," the guy answered; "I want to watch the 'experts at work' for a while."

He said that with quotation marks, in the jokingly ironic tone fishermen always employ in situations like this, but he was entirely serious.

The lake covered about ten or fifteen acres, plenty big enough for motorboat traffic, although there was no one on it at the moment. It was gourd-shaped, lying east to west with a south-westerly hook at the inlet end. Lazy hills with ponderosa pine trees sloped down to it on the west side, and some box elders and cottonwoods stood along the little stream that fed it. This was a regulation medium-to-large foothills reservoir gone half wild.

Most of the houses had been built at a respectful distance, so, with a few wooden docks lying out on the water and trees standing right to the shore, it did not look any more civilized than your normal resort lake.

At the moment it was dead calm and smooth, reproducing every nuthatch, pine needle, dock piling, and puffy, white cloud like a reflecting pool. A few odd trout were coming lazily to the surface here and there, making slow, flushing swirls. Not what you could accurately describe as even a sparse rise, just enough activity to illustrate that there were some fish in there.

A.K. and I waded in and began the professional-looking process of scanning the water for insects, finding only the occasional ant, beetle, and soggy box-elder bug. Not much of a rise, nothing much on the water. Ah, science.

Well, maybe later something would happen to give us a bearing, something like a caddis hatch, or a nice mayfly spinner fall. Anything would do; even a migration of water dogs would be better than nothing.

Meanwhile, the guy who'd invited us to come figure it out for him lounged under his tree like someone sitting patiently through the previews waiting for the movie to begin.

I shrugged at A.K. and dug out my you-gotta-start-somewhere fly, a #14 Hares Ear Soft Hackle. When A.K. saw that, he went to his streamer box and got out a big, juicy yellow marabou job. We didn't need a consultation to determine that neither of us knew what to do, but that we sure wouldn't catch anything if we didn't get some hooks in the water.

A.K. began casting to the stream inlet where, maybe, some trout would be lying, breathing the cool, dissolved oxygen and eating a bug now and then if one happened by. I started working

EXPERTIZING   51

the open water along the drop-off shelf where—again, maybe—
some trout would be halfheartedly cruising.

It occurred to me that, although A.K. and I do know a little bit
about trout fishing, this was a strange lake on a slow day and we
were no more or less likely to catch a fish there than anyone else.
I was glad I'd told the guy we'd "see what we can do," rather
than, "If anybody can catch 'em, we can."

But then, that's one of the cardinal rules of expertizing: always
leave the door open and the motor running.

———

Expertizing means acting like an expert. Not necessarily
being an expert, mind you, but *acting* like one. There's a
difference.

It's something we all slip into from time to time when we
realize that we know just a little bit more about fishing than the
person we're talking to or, worse yet, that we really don't know
any more, but the person is willing, for one reason or another, to
believe we do.

The symptoms are painfully obvious. When a question is
asked we clear our throats, square our shoulders, glance briefly
at the ceiling, and begin with, "Well now . . ." as if we're
consciously pulling our minds down from some great height.

Our answers are laced with complicated qualifications. They
ramble, they're never simple. Often they're so obscure they end
up being meaningless. But then, if you have to ask the question
in the first place you probably won't understand the answer,
right?

This is a terribly embarrassing thing to get caught at, but it's
still a real temptation, especially for people who are in the
business in some way, like guides, tackle shop clerks, manufacturers' reps, and, most notably, outdoor writers.

The writer's problem is compounded by the high regard in
which many people hold the written word. "It's true," you'll
sometimes hear, "I read it in a book." In some circles this is
better than having actually seen it with your own eyes. The

assumption is that if you write stories about fishing, you must know more about it than the guy who reads those stories. Of course the truth is, the thing you probably know a little more about isn't fishing, but writing.

And there's no real guarantee of that either.

The fallacy is further complicated by those writers who really *are* experts on the water. I'm talking about the ones who are so legendary now that you don't even have to use their last names. You know, like Lefty, Dave, Lee, and Joan. It's possible to get an article published in a magazine and suddenly find yourself in some very fast company.

At the risk of sounding defensive, there are times when this expert business is actually thrust upon you. I remember the first time someone at a party introduced me as an "expert fly-fisherman," or words to that effect. I'd never fished with the guy, so he didn't know firsthand if I even knew which end of the rod to hold, but I'd written these stories, you see.

Being normal, I said something like, "Aw shucks," and let it go. I wasn't exactly making a bundle writing and I figured a little public stroking amounted to a nontaxable fringe benefit.

It was a mistake.

By the time I finally got around to admitting, "Look, I'm actually just a writer" (or sometimes I'd say "journalist" to make it sound a little more like a real career), the damage had been done.

"What a guy," someone said, "a great fisherman and modest, too."

Then a local Trout Unlimited chapter asked me to give a program at one of their monthly meetings. Flattered, I put together twenty or thirty slides that were more or less in focus and headed down to the hall where, once again, I was introduced in embarrassingly glowing terms by a man wearing an Orvis tweed shooting jacket. I was deeply knowledgeable, he said, smart, cagey, a master fly-fisher. I had never fished with this guy either. I walked to the front of the room and looked out on dozens of familiar faces, fully half of whom knew the same streams I did and could fish circles around me blindfolded. They applauded.

This is much more profound than simple stage fright.

———

Naturally, the most effective way to expertize isn't to hold forth in front of an audience (unless you actually happen to be a genuine expert) but to do the exact opposite, that is, keep your mouth shut and just assume the pose. After all, we operate in a deeply traditional sport where there are accepted procedures for such things.

You know the pose. It begins with a sloppy, faded fishing hat with a wide, dark sweat mark, and an old vest, preferably with that gray stain on one of the pockets that dates you back to the days when Gehrke's Gink came in those little plastic tubs that leaked.

Waders, be they canvas or neoprene, must be faded and heavily patched.

It helps to drive around in an old, unwashed pickup truck (this gives the impression that you've been all over hell, mostly on dirt roads), and a beard with some gray in it is a nice touch. Luckily, the gray hairs have appeared naturally at my jowls (prematurely, of course), thus saving me from having to sneak into a beauty parlor in dark glasses to have the thing frosted.

As I said, you'll be keeping your mouth shut as much as possible, but when circumstances force you to speak, say very little and be as vague and enigmatic as possible. If that's hard for you to get a handle on, go down to the video store and rent some old Gary Cooper Westerns.

I've found that it's best to avoid facts and stick with opinions. Facts can be wrong, while the worst thing an opinion can be is weird. For that matter, a few off-center opinions can help to give you that impressive aura of unpredictability.

Try this: after landing several large browns, rub the back of your neck, suggest heading into town for a drink, and add, "Brown trout are a dirty, German fish, but brook trout need clean, clear water." That's a quote from novelist Craig Nova, but you can probably get away with it. Novelists—who, after all, are paid to have weird opinions—are almost always better to quote than straight fishing writers.

If you're trying for that aged, weathered effect that can be so convincing, slip a few dated words and phrases into your conversation. Refer to polarized fish finders as "smoked glasses," 7x monofilament as "fine gut," and remember that all cutthroats, regardless of race, are "Rocky Mountain speckled trout."

Note: you have to be at least forty to pull this off; fifty is better.

When theorizing is unavoidable, insist on doing it after the fact. Never predict how you'll do, but be prepared to explain later in great detail why you didn't catch fish, being careful to lay it on something that no one else was paying attention to, like the ozone content of the air or electromagnetic interference from satellites.

And never fall into that statistical macho trap that's so prevalent in fly-fishing these days. If you keep score, you can be beaten, but if you refuse to compete you can leave the impression that you have long since risen above that kind of crap. When someone says to you, "I caught forty-eight trout and ten of them were twenty inches or better. How'd you do?" say, "Yeah, we got some. Couple nice ones, too."

Another nice touch is to be much more excited about the blue herons and sandhill cranes you saw than about whatever fish you caught. This leaves the impression that catching trout is so easy for you it's a foregone conclusion. You hardly even notice it anymore.

Fish alone as much as possible. When you're with a group, wander slowly down to a bend in the river and then vanish into the trees. Don't come back for hours.

When you do return, remember that you are blissed out with solitude and a little distracted.

"Catch any fish?" they'll ask.

"Hm? Fish?" you say. "Oh yes, now that you mention it I *did* catch some fish."

When you're fishing within sight of other people, try to project a kind of aloof stillness. Spend long periods of time studying the water without casting. Find some rising trout, watch them carefully for twenty minutes, and then walk away, muttering to yourself, "Too small" or maybe, "Too easy."

Now sooner or later you'll catch a big trout in front of witnesses—if you put in enough time it's almost unavoidable—but remember that an expert remains cool and detached at all times; no whooping or hollering. Total ecstasy is expressed by allowing that, yes, it's a pretty good fish. The natural inference is that you've caught bigger ones, and lots of them.

The fact is, if you've been fishing for a number of years, and look it, people will assume you know what you're doing. All you have to do is keep from proving them wrong.

I'd advise against it, but if you really do want to set yourself up as an expert, all you have to do is stop talking about how you catch fish and begin referring to your "system." It works every time. And, as a well-known (and genuine) fly-fishing expert once told me, "Be damned careful what you say for fear of being believed. If you say you can catch more trout if you fish with your whanger hanging out, somebody will try it."

I rest my case.

———

A.K. and I fished our brains out on that private lake. We worked the inlet stream with wet flies and streamers. We fished large and small nymphs in the deep water over the drop-off using sinking lines. Then we cast to the shallow littoral shelves, then fished ants, beetles, and hoppers against the banks. I paddled the float tube into the deepest water I could find and trolled a big brown leech pattern. Then I switched to a bright yellow one thinking I could pull it out by catching a walleye.

Every fifteen or twenty minutes a heavy fish would wallow at the surface, always in a different place. Always in a different *kind* of place.

We tried everything we should have tried, but it was clear the real problem was simply how to put a single fly in front of a single fish on a big pond where precious few trout were showing themselves. It probably wouldn't have mattered much what fly it was, although I guess we'll never know for sure.

As any expert will tell you, this kind of thing happens from time to time.

After a number of passes by his shade tree, we finally convinced our host to get in his canoe and fish. That was right after we'd explained to him that the water was too warm, the sun was too bright, the barometer was too high, the air was too still, the moon was in the wrong phase, and there wasn't enough insect activity to really move the trout.

First the guy apologized for stringing up a spinning rod, saying he wasn't a good enough fly caster yet, but that he'd been taking lessons. Then he started casting a small, gold spinner in the general direction of the drop-off and retrieving it at a rate I'd have said was way too fast. I was going to say something about that, but decided against it, and it was a good thing because no more than ten minutes later he hooked a big rainbow that he played and landed beautifully, using a stern, but gentle hand. If it wasn't an honest twenty inches long, it was at least nineteen— a fat, handsome lake fish that any regular old blue-collar fisherman would be proud of.

It was also *the* fish of the day.

We went on casting until dark without another strike, and then the guy said something about being late for supper. There was no indication that anything normal, like a hot evening rise, was shaping up. Our host didn't offer to let us stay on without him, probably because fishing guests are required to be in the company of someone who belongs there.

When we left, the guy actually apologized for his trout, apparently convinced it had been an accident of some kind, and also still apparently convinced that A.K. and I were a lot better at this than he was. We had, after all, claimed to be experts, or at least we hadn't denied it.

Back at the front gate, I inspected the Touch-Tones and electric eyes, and I now think I know how an enterprising poacher could open the thing if he wanted to sneak in some night. Night fishing under the dark of the moon was the answer, we'd decided. Not that I'd actually do such a thing; it was just curiosity—a residual habit left over from a misspent youth.

CHAPTER 5

I'd Fish Anyone's St. Vrain

 A couple of years ago, just before leaving on what was shaping up, via long-distance telephone, to be a wild, rambling trip through Idaho and Montana, I told A.K. about a little stream a man had said he'd take me to—that is, if I could "spare a day amidst all the razzle-dazzle I had planned." Without mentioning its name, the guy had described it as a fair-to-middling creek that didn't hold any really big trout, but he said it was close to his home, real pretty, not too well known, and that he fished it a lot.

"It won't knock your socks off," he'd said, "but I think you'll enjoy it."

There *was* considerable razzle-dazzle planned, and the trip had taken on a life of its own with what was beginning to look like expeditionary proportions. In the end there were airplanes and rented cars, motels, lodges, guides, mackenzie boats, nearly as many big trout as the scheme had called for, a little bit of whooping it up, and a teeth-grinding ride from Bozeman to Island Park in a fast convertible with wire wheels and a Fuzz Buster.

And then there was going to be a day on this quiet little creek the name of which I would learn when I got there, if I decided to go. It sounded vaguely like the kind of fishing I claim to enjoy most.

A.K. wasn't coming along on this one, which seemed odd, but I was calling him out of habit every time a new piece of the itinerary began to solidify.

"Sounds like the St. Vrain," I said, and he replied, "I'd do it if I were you. I'd fish anyone's St. Vrain."

——

Most of the fishermen I know—even those who think of themselves as Sportsmen with a capital S—have a creek like this somewhere in their lives. It's not big, it's not great, it's not famous, certainly it's not fashionable, and therein lies its charm. It's an ordinary, run-of-the-mill trout stream where fly-fishing can be a casual affair rather than having to be a balls-to-the-wall adventure all the time. It's the place where, for once, you are *not* the tourist.

Even the guy in Idaho, who lives within day-trip range of some of the best trout rivers in North America, has this little creek tucked away somewhere. He can't brag about it in the usual extravigant terms, but he still likes to show it off to, as he put it, "the right people."

You naturally take that the way it was meant—as a combination involved compliment and fair warning.

My little creek is the St. Vrain. I've lived within sight of it for a long time now, and, even though people keep asking me why I don't move someplace where the fishing is better, like Montana, I'll probably live here unless (or until) it gets too crowded up in this end of the country. And that could happen, though it's not something I care to think about.

One reason I probably won't move is that I'm easily spoiled. There's no telling what kind of unyielding snot I'd become if my home water was the Madison.

I'd have to say that I more or less blundered into this situation, largely because I already knew the stream, and the property was cheap, but then I've apparently "blundered" into a number of things that have worked out rather well in the end, leaving me with the suspicion that there aren't as many legitimate accidents in life as there sometimes appear to be. That kind of thinking can get too new-age (and too easy) but it's still tantalizing: the thought that you have ended up exactly where you're supposed to be, and so maybe you can relax.

Granted, that's easier in some places than in others.

Profound relaxation kicks in when you find yourself able to satisfy one of your more acute cravings, like, for instance, the need to fly-fish for trout in a stream just about any time the mood strikes, and to occasionally even have some success at it.

Somehow it's most meaningful if this craving we're talking about has no practical reasons attached to it. Trout fishing where you return everything you catch to the water is a good example of that. Sex with careful birth control would be another.

The day I moved into this house on the creek—well, across the highway from the creek, actually, although it sounds better the other way—I knew that, in time, I would become deeply familiar with it, and that a lot of good things would flow from that. I had already invented a life for myself as a free-lance writer and trout bum–the bohemian equivalent of a country gentleman. By "invented" I mean that the blueprints were all drawn up, it was just a matter of actually building the thing using the materials at hand.

I was living with a girl then, and, if I'd been paying attention, I'd have noticed that her blueprints were a little different from mine, and also that this novel I'd written myself into had a hero who was single. But life is complex, and you can't keep an eye on everything. I say now that she and I were married. That's not technically correct, but I'll stand by it. When the lady moves out and you end up talking to her lawyer, you were married, papers or not.

I could also say she thought I spent too much time fishing, and that I sold too few stories for too little money. That wouldn't be entirely correct either, but it would be close enough.

—

For the first few seasons I fished the creek almost every day that I wasn't working or fishing somewhere else. I'll say, as humbly as possible, that I came to know it as well as anyone did. And it wasn't all that easy either. It's a small brown trout stream that does get fished some, and browns get funny about that. Even the little ones.

I really did come to know a few trout by their first names, as they say, caught some of them more than once, and felt bad when in early summer one of them was replaced in his usual lie by a different, smaller fish. That almost surely meant the bigger trout had died, and all I'd ever know for sure about that was, in most cases, I wasn't the one who killed him.

It was in the third or fourth season that I was sitting here at the desk trying to write a magazine story about how to do something or other with dry flies. I was straining to describe, both accurately and prettily, how the cast went, and then the drift, and then, if it all went well, how the fish would take said fly on said drift in said type of current. I was ripping pages out of the typewriter, wadding them up, and tossing them on the floor for the cat to play with.

Then I thought, What's wrong with you? Go across the street and *look at it*. That's what Al McClane would do.

I got the rod I kept by the front door, crossed the road in front of the house, walked up to the headgate, got in, waded up to a curl of current next to an exposed tree root, tied on the fly from the article, made the cast, and caught the ten-inch brown that I knew lived there.

Yes. Fantastic. It actually works. I was back at the desk typing in five minutes, my felt soles leaving temporary damp footprints on the rug.

The girl was gone by then. She'd have wanted me to leave my wet hip boots on the porch, I wouldn't have seen the necessity of that, and a distraction would have begun to take shape. Contrary to what some of my friends think, it's not marriage I'm against, it's just that maze of distractions that makes you feel like you're walking in knee-deep syrup.

So, of course, the arm has to go like this, and the fly lands like that, and there's the way the little bulging strip of water where the fish is has almost the same gnarly grain as the root of the black locust tree. Maybe it wasn't *War and Peace*, but I was getting words down on paper that might sell. With all the windows open on the hot, semiarid Colorado summer, the footprints would dry in an hour.

It was a moment when I realized I had something I'd always wanted, and, furthermore, that it had turned out to be something worth wanting for a change. Jesus Christ, was I happy.

———

Lately I haven't been fishing the creek as much as I used to. I'm not tired of it, I think it's just like that point you reach in a comfortable love affair where it's okay if you don't get it on every single night.

A number of things have happened since I've lived here.

There have been some fish kills. Some were the natural results of low water and rough winters, while the worst, of course, were human caused. The stream survived both kinds rather nicely in the end, both with and without help.

There were some seasons of environmental activism practiced at a level that can't be sustained forever without cracking up, which is a whole other story.

There were the special regulations that came, and then went, because the Division of Wildlife didn't think the creek was good enough to be included in the Gold Medal Fisheries program. And then *that* turned out to be okay because the annoying crowds of fishermen left as soon as the signs came down.

There was the staggeringly expensive Trout Unlimited–planned/Division of Wildlife–sponsored habitat improvement project with its attendant, hands-on lessons in hydrology, and the renaming of Walsh Pond as Walsh Riffle after a single high runoff. Trout streams have minds of their own, and I don't just mean that the trout can be snooty.

There was the spring when everyone got scared because the runoff was so high anyway, and then it started to rain in the high country up the drainage. It looked as if a flood was in the works.

Driving home from bluegill fishing one evening I came to a road block on Highway 36. The creek, normally about fifteen feet down there, was so swollen you couldn't have floated a #16 Adams under the bridge. The official opinion was, the bridge wasn't safe to drive across. It did seem to be vibrating a bit.

The cop wanted me to go around, and I said I lived right over there and was, by god, going to go home to check things out. It turned into something of a discussion and he asked me if I wanted to get my ass arrested. Without thinking, I took a step forward and asked the officer which side of the bridge he wanted to try to do that on.

He relented, which was nice of him, and let me cross at my own risk. I said I was sorry, which I was. Just in kind of a bad mood, you know? I think my house is about to wash away and I don't have flood insurance.

The story got around, as stories will, but in the end it only seemed to help my standing with a certain segment of the community. Maybe I had these literary presumptions, maybe my fishing tackle was too fancy, but anyone willing to duke it out with the police for no good reason must be a regular guy after all.

There's something about seeing a normally sleepy little creek swell up to within inches of bursting its banks like that. It seems to indicate that even long-term appearances can't be trusted. You spend a strangely pleasant all-nighter sitting on the railroad tracks with some neighbors drinking beer, watching what you can see of the water in the darkness, checking the level of it with a flashlight, reexamining how good an idea it is to live this close to a trout stream.

Later you wonder how the fish fared in all that. I mean, it was thick as stew, and tree trunks were floating in it. In the end there were some minor structural changes in the banks. Your house is still there, so now you can selfishly worry about the poor little trouts.

Still later, when the water has dropped and cleared, you find that they're right there as they always were—about the right number of fish, and in all the right places.

It might passingly occur to you, while changing dry flies, that you know how to catch these creatures in certain proscribed situations, but there's a hell of a lot more that you'll never understand. A.K., on the other hand, exhibits no surprise whatsoever. He releases the fish he's just landed and says, "Look, if high runoffs killed the trout in streams like this, by now there wouldn't *be* trout in streams like this, right?"

You can be amazed by it or not, it's up to you.

———

I don't fish the St. Vrain quite as often as I used to, or quite as hard either. After a number of seasons and lots and lots of brown trout, I've started to get distracted by things. Birds mostly, but other things, too.

Since I've lived here I have identified, in a loosely delineated piece of real estate that is seldom out of sight of the creek, exactly sixty-nine species of bird. The interesting part of that is, only one of those—the varied thrush—was of any real surprise to the ornithological types, and those people can get excited, let me tell you. All the rest belong here.

I've become a fairly serious birder myself now, complete with four guidebooks, a good pair of field glasses, and a fourteen-dollar-a-week feeding habit.

No, I won't list the birds for you. I was tempted there for a minute, but no. Not all sixty-nine.

I'll list the mammals, though: we have mule deer, elk (once in a blue moon), mountain lion, coyote, red fox, beaver, muskrat, fox squirrel, short-tailed weasel, yellowbelly marmot, raccoon, rock squirrel, prairie dog, Colorado chipmunk, porcupine, cottontail rabbit, black-tailed jackrabbit, and assorted, unspecified mice and voles that amount to generic owl food.

The great horned owls that are the most common along the creek eat their catch, and then regurgitate "owl balls": round, plum-sized gobs of hair and bone that look a lot like turds, but that technically are not. An owl will often do that day after day from the same roost, leaving a pile of balls on the ground. You find the spot when, one afternoon, you notice a bunch of magpies scolding an owl. You can break the balls open and see what the owl has been eating by the little skulls and teeth inside. It's fascinating, although I guess you actually have to be there to appreciate it.

This is not something you get into every day, certainly not when the fish are biting. More to the point, it's something I don't seem to have the time for anywhere else.

Of trout stream insects we have nineteen and counting, mostly known by the common names and hook sizes, but with some Latin by way of my friend Ken Iwamasa. Fly patterns are carried to imitate most of them.

For spiders and other terrestrial bugs I don't have a reliable count because I can't swear to the absolute accuracy of some of my identifications, and, frankly, don't look at them that closely if fish aren't eating them. There are lots of them, though, and I have gone to the trouble of keying out such terrestrial oddities as the Gila grasshopper.

A Gila grasshopper is flightless, and, as the name implies, is striped head to butt in alternating orange and black like the famous lizard. Preliminary chumming experiments indicate that brown trout don't care for them, and probably don't even know what they are. It's just as well. It wouldn't be an easy fly to tie.

Way up in the rocks where fishermen seldom go you can find what the field guide tells me is probably a lesser earless lizard. A big brown would probably eat one of these, but I don't know how it would get in the water.

Closer to the stream there are beautiful brownish-orange and green-striped plains garter snakes, gopher snakes—whose defense mechanism is to look like a rattler—and, of course, the impressive prairie rattlesnake itself.

I've always liked rattlesnakes for some reason, although I've never lost my respect for them and have, a time or two, killed them when they were coiled belligerently next to my front porch steps. Maybe to make up for that, I also once saved one.

I was walking over an irrigation headgate on the way to fish the Cement Plant run, when I noticed a nice big rattler struggling against the current where the main channel sluices off into the ditch. I don't know how long he'd been stuck in there, but he seemed very tired, and looked as if he would drown pretty soon. On about every third pathetic wiggle, his head would go under.

After deciding against using the bamboo fly rod, I found a good, long stick and fished him out. He lay there on the ground in loose coils for a few minutes, and then crawled off stiffly.

The guy I was fishing with didn't say much, but the look of horror on his face was clear enough. He didn't approve. I didn't know him very well, and never fished with him again after that, but he was surely the one who started the story that this crazy guy who lived by the creek was planting rattlesnakes down there to guard his favorite fishing spots.

When that tale came back to me a few weeks later I said, "Yeah, I know that guy. He's nuts." If someone wants to spread it around that your home water is dangerous to fish, you probably aren't required to go out of your way to correct the impression.

Botany is one of my many weak areas, but I'll say there are no fewer than eight species of tree along the lower stretch of creek, most deciduous, but with some ponderosa pine and juniper. There are also yucca and prickly pear cactus, plus who knows how many molds, mosses, shrubs, vines, weeds, grasses, herbs, grains, berries, wildflowers, and mushrooms. I suppose I could learn and list everything, but at some level that begins to seem pointless. Let's just say the soil is rich, black river bottom, and there's plenty of water, so it's very lush close to the creek.

Most of the exposed rock is, I believe, sandstone, and much of it is covered with various lichens. All I know about lichens is the folklore. The flaky black stuff is supposedly edible (I've never tried it) and the orange stuff is supposed to have an affinity for the urine of large game animals.

After a hard frost has made them wrinkly, the hips from the wild rose bushes make good tea. Lots of vitamin C. Good for colds. Lace it with Wild Turkey or Dickel.

There are chokecherries that can be made into a painfully tart jelly, or, better yet, mixed with something sweeter, like the raspberries.

Some springs I've found wild asparagus, thanks to the late, great Euell Gibbons, although usually I overlook it until it gets too big and woody to eat.

And, naturally, there are fish: dace, some suckers, lots of brown trout, the occasional rainbow, and once a single, confused-looking little bluegill. This, in fact, is the one advantage the fly caster has over your regulation binocular-toting, pith-helmeted amateur naturalist. Those guys never see the fish.

Yes, I have kept some notes, although it turns out that they're not very neat, and weren't all that easy to locate, having been scribbled on odd pieces of paper and stuck in various guidebooks.

I have lots of field guides, have taken to reading David Quammen religiously, and am slowly coming to appreciate the diversity of a single strip of riparian habitat by keeping rough lists in the old style. When it comes to naturalism, I stopped somewhere in the nineteenth century, back when some anthropomorphism was still allowed and the observer didn't have to remain completely objective.

And, of course, when someone with a real science background puts me on the spot I can say, "Gimme a break, I'm just a fly-fisherman."

I have learned a number of things about fly-fishing for trout here, too: the kind of sly, unlikely sort of things you learn when it doesn't matter if you catch anything today or not because you have all the time in the world. When you have the luxury of time you never have to decide if you're goofing off, or actually waiting the fish out. The results will be about the same.

These things—call them tactics or approaches—work on other streams, too, but never quite as well.

Watching birds and doing autopsies on owl balls notwithstanding, I *do* still know where some fish are, including some obscure spots hidden in between the obvious ones that any competent fly-fisher would wade right to on his first visit. Sometimes the reason why a trout is there becomes clear once you've hooked or seen him. Sometimes not. Nor are they entirely dependable.

Still, places like that accrete over the years, and finally begin to illustrate the stream's particular style. They don't quite fit together into a theory, but they end up heightening that sense you occasionally get that translates as, "I know where a trout is." If anything, A.K. is a little better at this than I am, at least on some days.

———

I didn't meet A.K. on the creek, nor did I introduce him to it—that would have been too perfect—but we've fished it together steadily for years through thick and thin, so that now it's our standard point of reference. Either of us knows precisely what the other means when a creek is described as "St. Vrain-like" or "twice the size of the St. Vrain" or "a little better than" or "not quite as good as."

"Like the St. Vrain, only with cutthroats" was a particularly good one.

And it's clear what "someone's St. Vrain" is, too. It's a stream you've heard of only in passing, if at all, where the fishing is easygoing—if not actually easy—and where the guy who's showing you around may seem to be ignoring the fishing while pointing out things like an otherwise ordinary-looking boulder where once, on a chilly September morning five years ago, a mountain lion materialized for a few seconds and then vanished like smoke.

This is a stream with what novelist Tom McGuane calls a "neutral reputation." There are some trout in it, you'll learn if you ask, and yes, people do fish it, but that's about it. If it was a real good one, you'd have heard of it, wouldn't you?

All over the West you see these things on maps and drive over them on two-lane concrete bridges. Generic trout streams that vanish too quickly in the rearview mirror. Somewhere there's a guy—more likely a handful of guys—who know as much as anyone about each of them.

I know from experience that showing someone the very boulder on which the lion was sighted is ridiculously anticlimactic, but it's still somehow unavoidable. The right people try to be courteous. They'll direct their attention to this gray rock, say, "Far out," and mean it as much as possible under the circumstances. After all, you can't expect someone to mess his waders over something that happened five years ago.

The same people will try to appreciate your vision of the place, even on days when the fishing is a little slow in the run where, you tell them, you once caught twenty-five browns without moving a step or changing flies. One of the nice things about being a local is that people are virtually required to believe what you say, if only because you were there and they weren't.

I know the St. Vrain is lousy with trout, even when, on the face of it, there's no reason to think that, so I catch myself saying what old-timers have said for generations: "Ooooh, they're in there."

———

Some years ago my teenaged nephew, Dan, was having some trouble, and he came out here to Colorado to visit his crazy uncle John, and to sort of work things out for himself. I was happy to do it. It had been done for me. This is what black sheep uncles are for, especially those who live on trout streams.

If the truth was known, this had been part of the original blueprint: to fish, write, live by the creek, and at around forty to have become the kind of man who'd have the proper distance on trouble.

Dan and I talked a little, mostly we fished, which is what he wanted to do. I was careful not to interrogate him because that had been done to me, too, and I didn't care for it. I thought, How bad could it be if the kid understands that he should go trout fishing and cool out?

The St. Vrain was being difficult then, and I suggested that we go find some easier fishing. But Dan didn't want that. He wanted the hard fishing, he liked it: was, in fact, fascinated by it. "This is radical," he said.

But he died anyway, not too long after that. Suicide. I had honestly thought everything was going to be okay.

Charley George used to fish the St. Vrain, and he's gone, too. Natural causes. Out in San Francisco where I had lost track of him. When I heard the news the first thing I said was, "I thought he was still in Arizona."

You always have to bring it back to yourself somehow.

Charley was a fine, good-humored minimalist poet. Not the kind who says very little, but the kind who says so much so well in so little space it leaves you giddy. His author's bio reads: "Charley George: writes for hire, fishes for trout, remains in debt."

See what I mean?

———

Dead friends and all the other accumulations. More than time, trout caught, or detailed lists, they're what make you an old-timer on a piece of water. More even than actually being old, or being able to remember when the fishing was better. They may also be why the old-timer isn't giggling happily every time you see him. You think he's a little dinged out, and maybe he is. He's carrying a fly rod, but he's just standing around smoking, or back in the trees watching birds. Maybe fishing has made the guy a little crazy. Maybe this is the one who plants the rattle-snakes.

Put him on a different stream and he'll seem perfectly normal.

———

Yes, I did fish the little creek with the man in Idaho. As he'd promised, it was small, pretty, fair to middling, and so on. The kind of unassuming little trout stream you wouldn't go to fish if you weren't damned near there already. It was a pleasant break toward the end of a trip that was, perhaps, a little on the frantic side.

I caught a few small trout from spots where, I was assured, other fishermen before me had caught more, and was shown where the elk came down every year, as well as the exact spot where my host had once dropped a five-point bull with a single, brilliant shot.

But I guess that doesn't make for much of a story.

CHAPTER 6

THE
LESS-lOVEd
FIShES

A few years ago I took a trip to one of those fly-in wilderness fishing camps in Canada's Northwest Territories—float planes, timber wolves, tundra, enormous fish, the whole bit. I packed a bundle of fly rods (from 4-weight to 9-weight), and it was in my mind to prove a point by catching all the available game fish—Mackinaws, northern pike, grayling, and lake whitefish—fairly on flies. Which I did, although I resorted to a spinning rod and jigs a few times when the lake trout were in deep water. I've yet to determine at what depth fly-fishing ceases to be feasible, but on that trip I established that seventy feet was definitely past the limit.

When I got home I was sunburned, tired, jet lagged, bug bit, five pounds lighter, and had a grocery bag full of exposed color film, plus notes for half a dozen magazine articles. That's when it got interesting.

The straight fly-fishing magazines wanted to hear about trout, salmon, and maybe bass, but *not* grayling or lake trout, certainly not pike, and some seemed offended that I'd even mention whitefish in the same paragraph with flies and fly rods.

Okay, fine. Some people just don't know a good story when they see it. There are other magazines.

Some of those other magazines, citing demographics, coldly

informed me that fly-fishermen catch trout, period, while guys who fish for Mackinaws and pike use live minnows or plugs, and the few whitefish specialists are into maggots. That's just the way it is, kid. And this, by the way, from editors who had told me before, and who have told me since, that they wanted stories for their magazines that were more than "just the same old stuff hashed over again."

One guy even gave me a list of fish he didn't think his readers cared to hear about: grayling, whitefish, arctic char, Dolly Vardens, and kokanee salmon.

One is left to assume, I suppose, that suckers and lamprey eels are off the list entirely.

I did finally manage to sell a few stories from that trip, and I can't say I wasn't already aware of the tendency of some fishermen and fishing magazines to look down their noses at "certain" fish. Still, it was the first time I'd run smack up against clearly stated, unmitigated chauvinism.

Of course, if you don't care for some fish—for whatever reason—you should leave them alone. There's no principle of fairness in operation here, and no fish will ever feel slighted if you choose not to pester him. After all, we're the ones who have all the fun at this. The fish actually don't like it much.

You should, in other words, do whatever you want, even to only fishing for indigenous brook trout with hackled Catskill-style dry flies in streams with rhododendrons blooming on their banks if that's what it takes to turn you on. After all, getting turned on is what this is all about.

For that matter, anyone who wants to turn his back on good fly-fishing has my blessing. It leaves things less crowded for those of us who'll happily fish for just about anything that swims, as long as it will eat a fly. Not to the exclusion of trout, but for variety, out of curiosity, and just because the fish are out there.

———

The first grayling I ever caught were in two high mountain lakes and a beaver pond in Colorado. All three of these places were hard to get to, but the fish themselves were pretty easy to find and catch, which seemed like a fair trade.

These are the kinds of places you can get used to when you live for years in this part of the country: heartbreakingly beautiful, but also ordinary. Between the grunting and sweating it takes to get up there, and then the fishing—which can engage all your attention—you can actually forget to even look at where you are. That is, until you catch a strange and wonderful fish you've never seen in the flesh before. There's nothing like a new fish for freshening a jaded outlook.

Grayling are an exotic fish here, and you'll only find them in a few places where they were introduced. It seems that back in the 1930s there was some concern for the future of the Montana grayling in its home state. Officials there were afraid it was about to follow the Michigan grayling into extinction, so they arranged to spread them out a little, and Colorado got some.

But, I'm told, Colorado trout purists didn't like them. They'd never seen grayling before and thought they were some kind of sucker with a big dorsal fin. It was quickly decided that grayling were too small, had soft mouths, didn't taste good, were too easy to catch, and competed unfairly with trout for the limited food supply in those high, cold lakes.

This, by the way, is the standard rap when fishermen are confronted with a new species. It's immediately seen as a no-good, bottom-sucking lobster that will infest and ruin every lake and river in the state inside of ten years: on a scale of catastrophes, just one or two notches down from the end of the world.

There was a time when they said things like that about brown trout—you know, that ugly, dirty, German fish that was too hard to catch.

I've fished for grayling in Colorado, Montana, and the Northwest Territories, and have come to like them a lot. If I read my ichthyology correctly, they're between trout and whitefish on the evolutionary scale. They're streamlined, handsomely, subtly colored, and have that fabulous high dorsal fin that is used in mating displays, and possibly in fighting with fishermen, although there are those who will argue with you about that.

Some of the ones I caught in Canada had a radiant, iridescent quality to them, so that they'd go from a kind of sparkly tan, to bluish purple, to silver as you turned them in the sun. Actually, they're all like that, it's just that the ones in the Northwest Territories were so big there was more of it per fish, so it was more impressive.

These are the best-loved of the less-loved fly rod fishes, probably because they're real pretty, even to having vaguely troutlike spots on them. Trout purists have been known to perk up some at the mention of grayling—especially big grayling. Still, certain fly-fishers say they wouldn't travel far to catch them.

Depending on which fish expert you talk to, there are either two species of grayling—the true arctic and the Montana (plus the now-extinct Michigan breed), or there's just the arctic with a range extending down into the lower forty-eight states. All I know for sure is, the ones in Canada jumped like mad, while the ones in the Rocky Mountains fight more like bluegills, staying in the water and using up all their juice right off the bat. It's a hard enough fight, but short and definitive, with the fisherman usually winning.

Grayling live in cold streams and lakes, eat insects, and are otherwise troutlike in their habits, except that they seem to me to be slightly more eager to rise to the dry fly. Some say that makes them stupid.

Some also say these fish are hard to hook and land because they have a "soft mouth." That myth came about because a grayling will often roll on a dry fly, that is, come up right next to it and then take it on the way down. When they do this at the end of a thirty-foot cast, you have to delay setting the hook for precisely one and one-half heartbeats. At greater or lesser ranges you have to adjust the pause up or down in increments of a hundredth of a second per foot. There's nothing to it.

—

Lake trout are primarily a deep-water fish, but they'll take a fly when they're close enough to the surface. In fact, they seem to do it enthusiastically, probably because they're not a standard fly rod quarry. They see lots of plugs and hardware in places where they're fished for heavily, but not that many fly patterns.

You can get them on streamers in the fall when they're up in the shallow water to spawn; you can get them on streamers again when they chase schools of bait fish to the surface and go into a classic feeding frenzy. On rare occasions you'll find them working to windblown shoals of floating insects or rising to caddis flies where a stream enters a lake.

In Canada I landed several in the eight- to ten-pound range on streamers—little fish to the guides, but by God ten-pounders on a fly rod to me.

I also hooked a hog on a dry fly. We were fishing for grayling in the river, and I had worked my way down to where the current spread out into a small lake. There was a big backwater down there with a thousand size 14 caddis flies floating on it and one enormous nose sucking them daintily, one by one, from the surface.

I cast to the fish, of course, and he took the little Elk Hair caddis casually. Remember, this was way back in the bushes and the poor thing had probably never seen a fly that wasn't real. He wiggled tentatively near the surface a few times, and I noted that the distance between his tail and his dorsal fin was roughly two feet. That's about two-thirds of the total length of a mac, and the head had been about the size of a grade-A large grapefruit.

I describe him in those terms now because that was the most I ever saw of him. He was hooked on a light rod, 5-weight line, and 5x tippet—a nice, sporting rig for grayling that might go three pounds, tops.

I don't think he ever realized what had happened to him, but he didn't like it, and apparently decided to swim over to the other side of the lake to think it over, in the process peeling off all my fly line and starting on the backing.

None of that took very long to happen, but I had time to realize I should have at least switched to a stouter leader and bigger fly, if not gone back to the boat for an altogether heavier rig; that this thing was easily longer than the biggest fish I'd ever hooked on a dry fly; also that I had not paid attention in grade school as I'd been told to; that I had sometimes not been kind to my friends; that the ultimate meaning of existence continued to elude me, and so on.

No more of my life would have flashed before my eyes if I'd been falling down an elevator shaft, and I never once thought, What the hell, it's only a lake trout.

———

On that same Canada trip I landed what probably would have been, at the time, a world fly rod record lake whitefish in the two-pound tippet class. It wasn't what you'd call a legendary fish, but the International Game Fish Association had just started keeping freshwater fly rod records then, and a lot of the slots, including lake whitefish, were still wide open.

It was a mistake, or, as I prefer to think of it now, an unscheduled adjustment. There was this really big fish rising in among a large pod of what had turned out to be two- to two-and-a-half-pound grayling. With that as a scale, he looked a good five pounds or more, and, with all that IGFA stuff in the air, I couldn't help recalling that the all-tackle world record grayling was right around five pounds.

Naturally, the fish was in a spot that required a long, accurate cast and a tough drift. It took half an hour to hook him and then quite awhile to land him on the light tippet, and, yes, I was a little disappointed that he wasn't a grayling. In fact, I seem to remember feeling downright cheated at the time.

It was sometime later that I realized it had been a fine, healthy, hefty fish that had taken a dry fly, fought nicely, and then lay there in the landing net looking handsome in a businesslike sort of way, much like the mountain whitefish I knew from back home, only fatter—and much bigger.

We had a good scale with us, but we didn't weigh the thing because it was only a whitefish. I'll stand by my guess of five pounds, though, maybe even closer to six. It wouldn't have been a record that would stand for years, but it would have gotten me into the book. For a season or two, it would have felt something like fame.

Around the West, fly-fishing types don't think much of the regional mountain whitefish. They crowd the trout, it's said, eating up the insects that would otherwise grow great big browns and rainbows. Well, maybe, although it's been my experience that the biggest whitefish live side by side in rivers that also hold the biggest trout.

The various divisions of wildlife all consider them to be honest game fish, but among anglers they often get lumped together with suckers in the "turd knocker" category. A similar label is sometimes attached to the fishermen who catch whitefish for food, and refer to them as "smokers."

On the Henry's Fork in Idaho I've seen fishermen who otherwise seemed reasonable strangle whitefish until they gurgled and then throw them back in the river to slowly die. "Squeeze-and-release fishing" they call it, with superior, know-it-all grins on their faces.

These, of course, are the same guys who will patiently resuscitate a trout before gently releasing it.

Three years ago on the Henry's Fork I spent a very pleasant evening catching eighteen- to twenty-inch-long whitefish on dry flies during a blizzard caddis hatch. It was pleasant, that is, except for the bodies of abused whitefish that kept drifting down from fishermen upstream and bumping into my legs.

Only two comments here: First, be consistent. If you're going to do things like that, then don't give me any of that crap about the "artistry of the sport" and "respect for the game and the environment," okay? If you want to be a brutal, wasteful clod, at least have the courage of your convictions.

And second, killing any game animal and then just letting it lie is illegal (look under "waste of meat" in the regulations) and some states offer rewards.

—

Longnose gar, *Lepisosteus osseus*. This is a prehistoric remnant of a fish that lives, among other places, in the Verdegris River in Kansas where my friend, Larry Pogreba, said he'd take me last April as soon as his source called to say the conditions were right. His source is one of those rich, doctor/fly-fishermen who catches these things with a fly rod, often from the comfort of a belly boat. He's a man who, the story goes, gave up bonefish and tarpon because the gar were bigger than the former, *as* big as some of the latter, and more fun than both put together.

All I could think to say when I heard that was, "No shit?"

A twenty- to twenty-two-inch longnose gar is a baby, maybe a year old. Keepers are measured in feet, and, as with all large, toothy fishes, there are unverified stories of attacks on domestic animals and humans.

This is a long, tubular fish with diamond-shaped scales; dorsal and anal fins large, and set too far back; beady eyes set too low on the skinny head; and a long, thin beak studded with small, needle-sharp teeth set in a perpetual evil grimace. It's your archetypal living fossil, by all accounts so big and horrible it's stunning.

And fight? Bring a heavy rod, spare lines, lots of backing, and maybe a stout club or big-bore sidearm.

The standard lure is a six-inch length of frayed braided nylon rope, fished like a streamer. The gar grabs it, and it becomes entagled in his tiny little teeth. Sometimes it holds long enough for you to land the fish. They say hooks don't work well because the beak is all bone, so even a heavy wire job with a fine point can slip out.

And I mean a piece of rope, period. No marabou wing, no turns of medium dun hackle at the throat, no hook. Old, well-used rope is best, the kind you'd find hanging on a nail in the barn or tangled up in the back of the pickup.

Just the other day I ran into a man who said he'd fished for longnose gar, so I asked him if there was an accepted way to catch them using an actual fishhook. He said, "Sure."

What you do is fashion a wire noose about as big around as the lid of a five-gallon pickle jar. Inside that you hang a light monofilament leader with a small hook on the end. Then you catch a little bluegill and stick it on the hook. The entire contraption is lowered into the river under a large red-and-white bobber.

I'm sure you can see it coming. When the gar eats the bluegill it sinks the bobber. That's your signal to tighten the noose around his beak and haul him in close enough that you can put a .357 magnum hollow point in his brain pan.

"That's not exactly what I had in mind," I said.

The International Game Fish Association will not consider a fish caught with nylon rope or a wire noose as a potential world record, presumably because no gentleman would fish like this and then admit it later.

The residents of Virgil, Kansas, home of the annual gar festival, don't seem to care about that. A length of rope fished on a fly rod is perfectly acceptable there. In fact, all methods are legal, with the exception of guns, and that only because there are too many people around during the festival. Someone could get plugged by accident.

Last year the trip fell through because longnose gar fishing conditions (one of the real backwaters of angling lore) were never quite right. This gar, they say, is a spring-spawning sight-feeder, so you need clear water in the month of May. It's about the same thing you're looking for if you're bluegill fishing, except that you could hook a fish as long as you are tall.

We're set up for this coming spring, though, and will be watching the Kansas weather reports. The river is known to go off-color easily in the spring rains and to take awhile to clear. The timing will have to be precise.

We'll bring some rope, just in case, and maybe a spool of braided wire, too, but the real project is to devise some kind of respectable streamer pattern, complete with a hook, that will work. That will have to be done on-site, so I'll be lugging along the portable flytying kit. Larry says he *has* caught these things on hooks by accident while bass fishing, so it can be done.

If we can manage it, and if we get into good-sized fish, the possibility of putting in for an IGFA tippet class fly rod record has not been ruled out, although I wouldn't say that's the real reason for going.

I guess if you have to ask, no reason would make much sense.

I figure I'll try writing about it, but when Larry voiced some concerns down at the café this morning over having the sport "popularized," I told him not to worry about it. For one thing, I can already see the rejection slips—"Let me get this straight, you caught *what* on a fly rod?"—and for another, I just can't picture mobs of serious fly-fishermen descending on Virgil, Kansas, loaded down with expensive graphite rods and dressed in official Tarponwear sport clothing.

On the outside chance it does become fashionable, Larry and I will be in on the ground floor. We could market stone-washed, prefaded, prepatched denim coveralls and make a bundle selling Garwear.

———

It was only last season that I caught my first kokanee salmon. These things are real salmon, but they're also largely plankton eaters, which makes them a little peculiar from a match-the-hatch perspective. Word was they could be taken by hook and line on a somewhat unpredictable basis, and none of the flytying books I've seen list a plankton emerger pattern, so I'd pretty much ignored them.

The accepted (and legal) method for kokes is snagging during the fall spawning runs, with generous bag limits rivaling those for panfish. Friends of mine had snagged them, and I had happily eaten some of the fish (which were excellent), but with a personal vision of myself as an old-school fly caster with a penchant for dry flies, I naturally considered myself above snagging, tickling, noodling, grappling, and all other forms of crude, ungentlemanly aggression against fish.

But then A.K. and I took off in October to fish a local trout river where, rumor had it, the Blue-winged Olive mayflies were hatching nicely. I was vaguely aware that there was a run of kokanees up this stream, and also that the snagging season was on, but I didn't think much about it until, in the course of stalking some rising rainbow trout, I came upon a pod of large, pink-sided, troutlike fish holding in a deep pool.

A friend had recently told me his favorite kokanee nymph was a Hares Ear, size 12, so I tied one of those on, added lead to the leader, and commenced to nymph fish.

I hooked the first three or four honestly in the mouth, proving it can be done. They were all between fourteen and sixteen inches, and fought sort of lazily, probably because they were pretty well whipped from the rigors of spawning. The males had hooked jaws with snarly teeth. They were sunken in the belly, but still had lots of meat on them.

I cut a forked willow branch and strung them up, remembering how they tasted brined and smoked over hardwood coals, and allowing as how they were headed off to die anyway.

I could stop there, with yet another example of a decent, cold-water fish that can be caught on flies, but I feel this urge to confess.

The fifth koke I snagged accidentally under a pectoral fin—as one will now and then do when nymphing to a hole with lots of fish in it—and I kept him, too, because, well, because there he was, and it was legal, and he was good to eat, and the limit was either twenty or thirty fish, I couldn't rightly remember. When you're a dyed-in-the-wool catch-and-release type, you don't pay much attention to bag limits.

By the time A.K. waded downstream to see what the hell was going on, I had ten fish on the willow stick, and had switched to a size 2 Wooly Bugger with six split shot ahead of it. That was as close as I could come to the regulation weighted, 3/0 treble snagging hook, known locally as a Texas Caddis.

"Are you catching those or snagging them?" A.K. asked.

"Uh, well, ah, the thing is . . ."

"I see," he said, and headed back up to the flat where real trout were rising daintily to mayflies. His false casts had a brisk, impatient look to them, like the swishing tail of an angry tomcat. But even a sportsman of A.K.'s stature had to break down when, sometime later, he found me lugging a four-foot-long stringer of twenty salmon that looked, from a distance, like a bunch of bananas. The bounty of autumn, free food with a long winter coming, and so on.

"Okay," he said, "how are you doing this?" and eventually we ended up on the bank cleaning a pile of forty fish and discussing whether or not a 5-weight split bamboo dry fly rod is the correct tool for snagging.

———

You're right, I got a little off the track there. Kokanees count as legitimate cold-water stream, fly-eating fish, but the method, legal though it may be, is still questionable, and I may or may not ever do it again. This one goes down in my list of lifetime experiences under the growing heading of "Ethical and/or Aesthetic Twilight Zone." At least with a piece of rope or a bluegill in a wire noose, the fish still has to swim over and eat it.

More to the point is the Colorado River squawfish. They're native to the drainage and once lived all over the western slope of the Rockies in Colorado. Now they're endangered—like so much else—and the Division of Wildlife has reintroduced them into a reservoir on the White River, with the usual cries of foul from area fisherpersons.

Some say they're a rough fish that will trash the more desirable trout in the river, thus ruining what passes for a tourist industry in a part of the state not really known as trout heaven. In this case it's probably true that the trout will suffer. According to *McClane's Standard Fishing Encyclopedia*, the diet of the highly predatory squawfish includes "young trout and salmon" along with just about everything else.

Some businessmen are also saying that, with an endangered

species of fish around, some bleeding-heart environmentalists will probably want to actually leave some water in the river, thereby screwing up diversions for development in a part of the state not known as growth heaven either.

The Division of Wildlife has patiently pointed out that squawfish were once considered a game fish back in the old days, and that they historically grew to lengths of four feet and weights of eighty pounds.

That sounds impressive, but for some reason no one is getting too excited about it.

And it doesn't help to know that a squawfish is a kind of minnow. Granted, it's a big one with "pikelike" habits, but it's still just a hyperthyroid baitfish.

So far I've kept my mouth shut on this one because it puts me in an uncomfortable position. On the one hand, I think trout streams should *stay* trout streams on the general principle that there are few enough of them as it is. On the other hand, the squawfish is native to the waters in question, while the rainbow and brown trout are not. As a member of the loosely defined environmental community, I firmly believe that the things that were here first demand some respect—to put it simply.

What I'll do is go fish for them in a couple of seasons when many have grown to the two-and-one-half-foot length the division guys say should be typical.

The illustrations I've seen of squawfish make them look awfully plain. Picture a standard bait shop minnow—gray to silver, a bit darker on the back—that is nearly a yard long. Possibly the largest fish most Coloradoans will ever catch in a river, but also probably one you wouldn't stuff and hang over the mantel in the den.

It's entirely possible that the nearby small towns of Rangely and Meeker will never get into a battle over which of them rates the title "Squawfish Capital of the Rocky Mountain West."

On the other hand, these things are fish—potentially very big fish—that can probably be caught on a fly. By all accounts, they should be suckers (no pun intended) for big streamers.

CHAPTER 7
STICKS

 I just received my first outdoor sports-related injury of the season. I was crashing around in some thick underbrush in the grove of trees behind the house and somehow managed to drive a long black locust thorn into my ankle. It could have been avoided if I'd been wearing boots instead of tennis shoes, but you know how that is. It was just fifty yards from the back door. I mean, it wasn't an *expedition* or anything.

I was going to write it off as a normal scrape, but by morning it was infected and I had to make a trip to town for a tetanus booster and a short lecture from the doctor about acting my age, which I thought I'd been doing.

Chances are I'll live.

What was I doing crashing around in the brush? I was cutting walking sticks. Every year I try to put in three or four good ones; not like those you pick up here and there as they're needed that are always too long, too short, too heavy, too light, too crooked, or so rotten they break. I mean "perfect" sticks that are a little better than elbow high, smooth, reasonably straight, seasoned and stout—but not too heavy. The sticks you always look for when you need one, but can never find. I try to keep a few leaning against the woodpile on the front porch and another one handy in the back of the pickup.

Why three or four? Because they have this tendency to disappear.

You'll be out hiking and will come to a place where you need both hands to climb some rocks, so you leave the stick where you can find it later. But then you come back a different way and don't go out of your way to look for it. After all, it's just a stick. The woods are full of sticks, right?

Maybe you use it as a wading staff while fishing a rough stream and, coming back a different way again, leave it lying on the far bank. Or maybe it just floats away while you're not looking. A stick will do that.

That's happened to me so many times that I now carry a length of decoy anchor cord with a dog leash clip on one end as part of my normal fishing gear. The clip fastens to a D ring on the fly vest and the loose end gets tied to the stick—either the one I brought or the one I went to find when I saw how fast the water was.

Last year I gave a stick to a friend who was having trouble wading trout streams because of a bad knee. I liked his attitude. He didn't say he couldn't fish in certain places, he said he thought he needed a stick in order to forge ahead.

"Here's one," I said.

That's where the three I cut last year went.

I guess I was afraid my friend would actually go out and *buy* a walking stick, something my late father would not have believed possible. By thumbing through this year's stack of mail-order catalogs, I have determined that you can pay anywhere from $24.95 to $85.00 for a walking stick or "wading staff," which is the aquatic version of the same item. The two are largely interchangeable, although if it has a lanyard on it, it's probably a wading staff.

Your basic commercial stick is made of hardwood, usually ash, and has a cord grip. Of course, we're not talking about just any old branch here, not for $24.95. This is "select" ash that is, in some cases, "correctly tapered to eliminate vibrations in heavy current." I am sometimes bothered by those pesky vibrations in heavy current (as much in the legs as in the stick) but then none of my sticks have ever been correctly tapered. They've always come in whatever haphazard way the tree decided to make them.

The wood business can get a little effete at times. One company pointedly *does not* tell you what kind of wood it uses—the implication being that it's cocobolo rather than pine— forgets the cord handle and jacks the price to $39.95. For some unspecified reason, only a limited number of these are available.

On the high-tech end is the now-famous Folstaff. This is a wading staff made from sections of aluminum tubing that fit together like tent poles and have an elastic cord running down the middle of them. The staff pops apart and folds up to be carried in a holster on the fisherman's hip. When he feels the need for a stick—unless it's one of those very sudden and surprising needs—he simply unholsters the thing, gives it a wiggle, and it "instantly springs and locks into a sturdy staff."

This is a neat gadget and I like it, in spite of my usual aversion to space-age outdoor gear, although it's not what I'd call a "stick" in the finest sense of the word.

A.K. uses one of these and swears by it, although at the end of some days I've had to help him pull the sections apart.

If the Folstaff is the ultimate in practicality, the Heritage Bamboo Wading Staff is the ultimate in class. This thing is made from tonkin cane, like a fly rod, and features a "jewel-like polished brass thumb crotch" and a "distinctive cast bronze rock gripping tip featuring the classic brush hook."

I like this one, too, although the price is a bit daunting at eighty-five dollars. Still, if a guy wanted to spend a lot of money to make himself a formidably snazzy fly-fisher, he'd have to buy one.

I've never personally felt the need to hook any brush while fishing, although I might if I had the cast bronze wherewithal to do so.

On the other hand, I can't shake the feeling that a stick—I mean a *stick*, after all—is one of the few things left in life that should be, and in fact is, free for the taking. Collecting a stick in the field is both harmless and satisfying. As a nonconsumptive use of the countryside it's just a hair below bird-watching and photography, but well above hunting, fishing, and fire building. And you don't need a license or a wood-gathering permit unless you're hauling them out by the cord for resale.

When you're out in the woods or walking along a trout stream, picking up a stick seems like such a natural thing to do: almost automatic. It's not always clear what you'll need it for, but you'll use it to pace your step, to lean on, or maybe to turn over a rock and poke the garter snake you find underneath. Whatever, when you see a good one you take it because it's the basic, ancestral tool. It feels good in the hand because it's the thing we're genetically programmed to wrap our unique thumbs around.

The stick was one of the first two tools (the rock being the other) and, as a lever, it was one of the early concepts. "Give me a fulcrum and a long enough lever, and I can move the world," someone in a grandiose mood once said. It's probably fair to say that any device that has a handle began its career as a convenient stick.

Like the fishing pole, for instance. A pole is a version of the stick, as are the shaft, rod, beam, stem, wand, and so on. We don't have as many words for sticks as Eskimos have for snow, but we do have a few.

No one knows for sure, but I'd guarantee that the first fishing pole was a found object. Some guy working a wooded stream with a hand line looked around and said to himself, "Give me a stick long enough and I can catch that sucker on the far bank."

Even a fly rod is basically a stick. In fact, that's what you'll call it if you're properly hip. After trying one out, you might say, "That's one radical stick, man."

———

It was my late father who introduced me to sticks. Whenever we'd go for a stroll in the woods, as we did often when I was a little kid, Dad would always stop within the first hundred yards or so and get a stick. Usually he'd just pick one up, sometimes he'd take out a sheath knife and cut one, but there was always a professional-looking process of selection to it. He'd look at it, wiggle it, sight down it, plant it on the ground, and firm it there. Then he'd nod in approval and we'd set off on the walk proper. With a stick in hand, Dad's gait took on some of the aspects of a swagger.

I didn't quite understand what Dad was doing then (just some kind of grown-up weirdness, I figured) but I think I do now. A stick for casual walking or wading should have the proper heft, feel, and weight; what amounts to the right style. It's a personal matter. You might like a heavier stick than I do, while I might like a longer one than yours. You might insist on near-perfect straightness, while I may be able to live with—or even prefer—a gentle, parabolic, straight-from-the-tree bow in mine. There are damned few straight lines in nature.

I like a smooth stick, but I can handle the butts of broken-off twigs unless I happen to be fly-fishing. In that situation the stick and the fly line both lie downstream where one invariably gets tangled in the other. Chances are you won't notice this until you get a nice fish on.

The criteria for selecting a good stick are subtle, but whatever you want, there's one out there in the woods right now that's perfect, as if it were grown just for you.

This year I got as fancy as I ever hope to get with a stick. Of the four I cut the day I hurt my ankle, one was clearly the best. It's a fairly straight piece of box elder ("select" box elder, that is) with a distinctive bow at the top that curves elegantly into a rough, gnarly knot which is the found-object equivalent of a silver boar's head. In a fit of nothing-better-to-do, I shaved the bark off and wrapped on a cord grip.

It's quite handsome, I think. If it were shorter and a bit stouter, it might pass for a knobkerrie (a weapon with one knobbed end). Longer and thinner would make it a staff. A friend called it a shillelagh, but a true shillelagh would have to be made of either oak or blackthorn to be absolutely authentic.

A shillelagh is also considered to be something of a weapon, and so far I have only leaned on mine, although in the months to come I'll probably rest the butt of a *.22* pistol on it to steady my aim. The knot on the end is for decoration, but I suppose it would come in handy if I decided to give something a sound whop. A good walking stick is harmlessly pastoral in appearance, but still has the faint air of weaponry about it.

Mostly this is just a simple device to keep me from washing downstream when I go trout fishing.

I did injure myself while getting this stick—the best ones always seem to be way back in the brambles—and that could be a bad sign. We outdoorsmen can't help but believe in certain kinds of magic, although we call it "luck" now, and it could be that the thing contains a certain medicine. Time will tell. If bad luck dogs my walks with it, I'll pitch it in the river, peeled bark, cord handle, and all.

In fact, I may have violated one of the main precepts of walking sticks by trying to make this one more or less permanent. For all of Dad's careful selection and obvious enjoyment of his sticks, he'd toss them at the end of the hike without even looking to see where they landed. It was an early hint that some things in life—good things, too—were expendable by nature.

Then again, in his later years Dad had a stick that lasted a long time. It was just a dog walking stick, and the dog, also in his later years, walked mostly on suburban streets. He still kept his nose to the ground, but I think he'd forgotten what he was supposed to be looking for.

The stick was a beautiful, cane-length piece of wood cut from a Chinese corkscrew willow tree: the kind of stick you'd expect to see in the hands of a gnome. Dad used it not so much to lean on as to poke things and sometimes to whack a big dog that tried to hassle Sam, the retired, white-muzzled beagle.

I came to associate that stick with my father and I wouldn't mind having it now as a keepsake, but, like all his sticks, it, too, disappeared somewhere along the line. It could be that, sooner or later, everything disappears.

CHAPTER 8

THE DROUGHT YEAR

 At two-thirty in the afternoon A.K.'s stream thermometer, hanging in the shade of the tent, registered 102 degrees. That was at the campground in Last Chance, Idaho, a town I'd always thought of as high, northern, and cool. It was the first week in August 1988.

That morning, sometime before dawn, it had been 31 degrees by the same thermometer. The cold felt wonderful as we cooked up a big breakfast and coffee on the Coleman stove, warming our hands first over the burners and then around the tin cups, but we knew what we were in for. For one thing, there was no frost because the air was too dry.

You move fast on a brisk morning, and we were up, fed, and out quickly. By sunrise we'd parked the trucks at Osborn Bridge and were already hiking up the river.

The wool sweaters and millar mitts came off shortly after the sun was up, and we were squinting and sweating by nine-thirty when the Callibaetis mayfly spinner fall should have started, but wouldn't. Not in that heat and piercing sunlight. That's why we were up so early in the first place. We were hoping the water in the Henry's Fork had cooled overnight and that the fish would be more active early.

They were not.

Technically, the explanation would come in terms of a long-term lack of cloud cover and air temperatures as much as 15 degrees above normal interfacing with the negative phototropism and upper temperature avoidance levels of rainbow trout and populations of various invertebrate aquatic food organisms. That's how some fly-fishermen on the Henry's Fork talk, and I'll admit that some things don't sound quite as bad if you use enough words to describe them. Luckily though, there are still a few guys around who will look you straight in the eye and say, eloquently and to the point, "It's been too goddamned hot for too long and the river has gone off."

We had arrived fresh and confident after blasting across Wyoming in A.K.'s air-conditioned pickup, and we'd fished hard, getting out earlier and earlier, staying out later and later, hoping that the weather had just displaced the clockwork of the hatches a little, that the timing was just different, and somewhere, sometime, the bugs were appearing and the fish were feeding.

But no. Unless it was in the stone-cold dead of night while we slept, it was not happening. We put in the long days and we put out the requisite brave, positive attitude, but the seams in the fabric of things that a persistent fisherman can usually slip through had melted shut in the heat. After a couple of days we'd landed only the occasional small trout.

—

For those first days, "we" consisted of A.K., Bob Fairchild, and me. According to plan, Jim Pruett met us later at the campground after stopping off to fish a little stream in Wyoming with his brother. He found the tent and the pickup out in the open, looking deserted in the blazing sunlight, and then followed our voices back into the shade of the trees where we were sitting with our shirts off drinking beer and passing the time by watching a dragonfly catch midges out of the air. As near as we could tell, the dragonfly was nailing about one bug out of five.

Jim was mopping his brow with a bandana. He'd just driven

over from Lander, and when the breeze from the moving truck stopped, the full weight of the heat landed on him. He looked a little dazed.

Our fishing report was brief and to the point: slow in the mornings, slow in the evenings, and *real slow* through the middle of the day. Would you care for a beer?

That kind of forced brevity is a clear sign of fishermen fending off a bad mood.

In the backs of all our minds we'd sort of known what to expect from that country before we even left Colorado. This was, after all, the famous drought and forest fire year. The Southern Idaho/Montana/Yellowstone Park part of the world had started it off way back in the previous winter with dusty little snowfalls that were pitifully below normal, continuing into the summer with temperatures that were way too high. The day we arrived in Last Chance there hadn't been a drop of rain in two months.

We had suspicions about what to expect because, smart fishermen that we are, we had contacted some people in the area to check on the conditions.

From friends we heard that the fishing "could be slow" but that it was not exactly what you'd call "lousy."

"Is it worth coming?" we asked.

"That's up to you guys," they said carefully.

The tackle shop owners sounded a little more ominous. When we asked, "Is the fishing any good?" we heard things like, "Well, there's water in the rivers, and there are fish in the water . . ."

You have to watch out for that kind of obfuscation. The correct answer is, "Yes, the fishing is good," period. If the voice on the phone can't say that, something is up. Fly shop types are never vague when the fish are biting.

Conflicting early predictions had started trickling in from Montana sources—informed and otherwise—as early as late March when the hope for anything like a normal snowpack had given out: it was going to be shitty, it was going to be just fine, and just about everything in between. You could take your pick, depending on what you wanted to hear.

In June, when the drought had settled in, the temperatures were breaking records, and the first fires were burning, one guide service sent out a newsletter saying, "Come on up, don't believe what you've heard, it's not all that bad," which, naturally, increased the level of suspicion.

"Not all that bad" is a pretty flimsy endorsement.

Early in the summer we had seriously considered canceling the annual trip to Idaho and Montana. "Think of the fishing we could do around home in the same amount of time," we said to each other, "and at less trouble and expense, too. No out of state licenses, no ten-hour drive across Wyoming."

Colorado had been unseasonably hot and dry that year, but it was off the western end of the official Weather Service drought map. Precipitation was down, but various official spokespersons were saying it was nothing to worry about. We took that to mean there *was* something to worry about, and they just weren't letting us in on it yet. Still, the trout fishing had started early because there wasn't much of a spring runoff, and it had been good, period.

But then, toward early July, it began to hit us that this was the pilgrimage we were talking about not going on: the trip north without which no fishing season in recent memory had been complete.

The expedition to Montana and the surrounding neighborhood is a regional tradition here in Colorado. People in other parts of the country sometimes assume that those of us who live close to it have become a little blasé, but it's actually the other way around. That country is like a planet of its own, and the closer you live to it, the greater the pull.

Jim, A.K., and I finally convened a committee meeting. The streams weren't crowded, we'd heard, and that sounded good. We also figured that the trout were still in the water as the guy said (we hadn't yet heard about the fish kill on the Madison River), and if they were in there they were eating, and if they were eating they could be caught. Logic. Maybe it wouldn't be great, but how bad could it be? Enlightened sportsmen like us could deal with it.

A few days later A.K. invited Bob Fairchild, his old fishing buddy from Michigan who had never fished the fabled Northern Rockies, to join up. Bob had heard the rumors, too, but, victimized by the mythology that surrounds "local" fishermen, he figured we knew something he didn't.

For the record, none of us actually came out and said that, did we, Bob?

So it was settled: once Jim joined us at Last Chance, we'd be a somewhat cumbersome—but still hopeful—two-truck, two-tent, four-man convoy with enough fly tackle to start a small shop. The itinerary was open at both ends. We'd go where we had to.

That meeting, by the way, took place in a bar called Murphy's, as in Murphy's Law. The law was even up on the wall in there: "Whatever can go wrong will." Outdoorsmen are supposed to be able to read the omens, but we all missed that one. Too obvious, I guess.

———

Last Chance was relatively deserted, as I've come to expect it to be in August with the famous Salmon Fly and Green Drake hatches over, and the Mahogany Duns and tiny Blue Quills waiting, as usual, for the chilly mornings of September and October. That's why we go then, to dodge the crowds. It was deserted, and dry, and hot as all get out, as I think I've already mentioned. The guy who runs the campground wasn't doing much business and he'd gotten sullen. He's a crank at the best of times; by August he was approaching being a pain in the ass.

And, of course, Yellowstone was burning. There were eight major fires going in the park, and some were creeping out into parts of Idaho, Montana, and Wyoming. You couldn't talk to anyone without hearing the latest rumor. The North Fork Fire (they'd given them all names by then) had alone burned a hundred thousand acres, and was currently moving at the rate of five thousand acres per hour; the south entrance to the park was closed, tourists were being turned away, and so on.

We were camped in a part of the world that was making the national news almost every evening.

The sky to the north was full of smoke. At night the moon came up orange through it, and by day the convection columns of it topped out at the height of thunderheads, looking like mushroom clouds from nuclear explosions. The comparison was unavoidable, especially in that heat.

In three days of hard fishing on the Henry's Fork there was one sparse, but passable, Callibaetis spinner fall, during which A.K. landed one good fish—the regulation Henry's Fork twenty-inch rainbow. I, for one, tried not to hold it against him.

We took to lounging in the trees behind the camp during the heat of the day, and there was considerable sitting and standing around on the river as well, waiting for something to happen, and entertaining the growing certainty that it wouldn't.

We were soaking our hats in the river to keep our heads cool. I badly sunburned the backs of my hands.

One afternoon Jim and I agreed that all streams make a distinctive sound, and that the Henry's Fork sort of sucked. The next morning we broke camp and headed up toward the smoke on the northern horizon. Some fire fighters we'd run into had told us the west entrance to the park was still open, and you could still get to the Yellowstone.

———

The days that followed stick in my mind now as a montage of driving, following leads, playing hunches, and generally catching only the odd, small fish in some of the finest trout waters in the western United States.

It was deadly hot, everything was on fire, and there seemed to be a collective bad mood building among stunned tourists, slightly panicked locals, and disgruntled fishermen.

The serious, high-pressure, "negative phototropism" types were even grimmer than usual. A group of them would grumble

and whine about fish while bolting breakfast in a café somewhere, planning yet another strategy. Then one of them would
say, "Okay, boys, let's go rip some lips," and they'd stalk out on
another patrol. I suspect some children who were on family
vacations to that part of the country went home and told their
friends, "It was weird. There's a bunch of middle-aged men up
there who hate trout."

At one point I found a rustic wooden phone booth in a
campground on the Yellowstone River and, with nothing much
going on in the fishing department, I decided to call my
girlfriend, Susan, who was visiting her mother in Michigan.

I told her that it was too hot; that I was standing in the smoke
from a huge forest fire; that the sun was red and the sky was kind
of brown; and that, although Robert Traver says he fishes in part
because there are no telephones on trout streams, I was nonetheless calling directly from the Yellowstone River, where the
trout were not biting.

She said it was hotter than that in Charlevoix, and humid to
boot, and she had caught only one small bass in a week. The
annual family fish fry was a few days off and they didn't have
enough fish to feed everyone.

She's a sweet girl, but sometimes she can be a little stingy
with the sympathy.

None of us had done very well on the Yellowstone. The
hatches were sparse, and the few cutthroats we saw seemed
stunned. I knew things were getting strained with the crew
when no one gave me any of the usual good-natured grief for
checking in with the lady. A.K., at least, should have made some
pointed comment about how I suddenly had this ring in my
nose, or words to that effect. Like several of my other married
friends, he feels he has a certain investment in my singleness.

Another bad sign was all the talk about how the places we
were fishing had been so much better in years past. There was
the blanket spinner fall on the Henry's Fork when we caught all
the big trout with not a single other fisherman in sight for days
at a time. And the same thing on the Yellowstone a few miles
below Buffalo Ford, except that was a Flavalinia hatch.

Fairchild listened to all this without comment. He knew it could be good. He'd been hearing about it for twenty-some years.

I guess there was a point when I, for one, was just going through the motions, fishing for no other reason than that I was there, and what else was I going to do?

This does happen, you get skunked, and you're supposed to take it like a man—if you can still say it like that. I mean, all of us except Fairchild had fished gloriously in that country in seasons past, catching big trout and lots of them, and this was the other side of it. There is always another side.

It's like poker. Winning is preferable, but you play to *play*. The money is symbolic, even when you come home just before dawn one morning, having lost the rent money, preparing yourself for the moment when your female roommate instantly becomes a hostile stranger without so much as a trace of humor. *You* know the loss is a matter of sport, and therefore not real, but *she* won't believe that, and in the heat of things you may come to doubt it yourself for a time. It's four-thirty in the morning, you're tired, a little high, and you're trying to explain the difference between total doom and controlled chaos to an unsympathetic audience.

Not catching fish is a little like that.

It's probably just a coincidence that face cards are pretty in the same gaudy way that trout are: that even a busted flush reminds me of a nice stringer of brookies. I'm a better fisherman than a poker player, but I do them both simply to see the thing unfold.

The point, you must remind yourself, is that it will not, and should not, unfold the same way all the time. If it did it wouldn't be any fun.

———

We collectively lost our sense of humor late one night at the Swan Creek campground, and held a second committee meeting where some grievances were voiced having to do with both the itinerary and the finances. Of course, the act of impaneling a committee in the first place means that the problem at hand is already insoluble. The only firm decision we came to was that a good fishing unit consists of two guys, one fast truck, and one tent—an operation too small to require either a treasurer or a sergeant-at-arms. Luckily, we got through it with no blows struck and really only a handful of ill-chosen words that have since all been taken back or forgotten.

I slept in Jim's new, futuristic dome tent that night, and when I had to get up in the dark to pee (having had a little to drink), I couldn't find the goddamned door because there were no discernible front, back, or sides to the thing. I came quite close to using the pocketknife to get out, but I didn't know exactly where the knife was either.

I remember thinking, This is not the fun part.

All in all, as A.K. always says, "The *fishing* was good, it's the *catching* that was poor." As with most things that someone always says, it was beginning to wear a little thin.

———

Whatever else you got yourself into, one thing you'd end up doing if you were in, let's say, West Yellowstone, Montana, in August of '88 was to develop an opinion on the fires in particular and on the relationship of humans to nature in general. Not only that, you'd be called upon to defend it. There were enough philosophical discussions going on that the place came off as a sort of Athens on the Fire Hole.

I was among those already armed with what I'll call the preservationist view: leave it alone, it's fine the way it is. Interestingly enough, that's also the position used by the Park Service to justify their let-burn policy on naturally caused fires. At this writing, less than a year after the fact, it's the one that has surfaced in the press, too: "Relax, folks, Yellowstone Park did not, in fact, burn to the ground, or, rather, it did, but it was supposed to."

I'd never before thought of the United States Park Service as

a gang of woodsy mystics, but here, roughly, is their position.
Judge for yourself.

We like to see nature as this perfect, perpetual motion
machine that just hums along forever, neat, tidy, and dignified,
but on a day in, day out basis it's a messy and violent business.

There'll be awhile when trees grow, and the forests spread.
That's nice for animals that live in the woods (and also for people
who think of trees as monuments), but not so nice for those that
graze on the shrinking grasslands. And the lodgepole pines
deplete the soil, too.

Then there will come a time when the woods themselves are
past their prime, and trees cover more than what might be
described as their fair share of the landscape, although that
might be too human an idea to insert here.

Then lightning strikes. It starts a fire because there's fuel for
a fire, and it's a big one because there's lots and lots of fuel.
Then the whole shebang burns up.

Maybe it burns until heavy snows put it out. Maybe it
smolders in the duff all winter and blazes up again the following
year. Whatever, it somehow always stops short of burning up the
whole world.

Then, suddenly, where there were once forests there are now
meadows; the wood ash replenishes the soil; grass appears;
grazing animals—like, say, buffalo—eat the grass, get fat, and
increase in numbers, while forest creatures, like, say, wood-
peckers—are a little thin for a while.

Then the trees begin to encroach again (the pinecones having
seeded nicely when they were toasted by the fires) and it comes
back around the other way again without missing a beat.

It's the perfectly ordinary ebb and flow of nature, and the only
problems are our own. We are inconvenienced some by it, and
maybe a little bit frightened. Poor things. In the end it's just the
way things are, and it's really quite beautiful—especially when it
happens in someone else's backyard, and they're the ones who
have to evacuate.

Okay, that might not pass as the official Park Service position, but it's surprisingly close. The only real difference is, they have to cover their backs more carefully than I do.

The fires didn't have a lot to do with the somewhat poor fishing that August, although they were tied in with it, as these things always are. The hot weather and unusually dry conditions were what made the fires bigger and more numerous than usual, and they were also what lowered the flows in the streams and warmed the water a bit too much, putting the trout fishing off for a while. I've only been able to find two reports of the fires directly killing trout. In one, the flames actually heated the water to fatal levels for the fish in a small, tributary stream. In the other, fish died when planes dropped fire retardant chemicals on them.

There were a few other scattered fish kills in the area, but they have been attributed to the low water.

In the spring there may be some deposition of ash in some streams—especially if the thaw is quick and heavy, and especially on streams with steep banks—but in the end the streams will probably be fine. There's one prediction that says the wood ash, acting as fertilizer, will mean some streams will receive more organic matter than usual (or a "spike of nitrogen") and will probably be richer than they were before, at least for a season or two.

Wildlife watchers are happy because the habitat for the big, impressive grazing animals, like buffalo, elk, and deer, will be better than it's been in recent memory. There will be lots of animals to look at, they'll be in good condition, and there won't be a bunch of trees in the way either.

A friend of mine who's a mushroom hunter says his club is already planning a massive invasion of the area for next year because morels get positively giddy in the soil of freshly burned forests. By the way, if you think fly-fisherman are unusual, talk to a mushroom hunter sometime.

There were fears for the local tourist economy, which was actually down noticeably late in the summer of '88, but even with the fires still in full bloom the Park Service was treating

them as an attraction by handing out hastily printed flyers titled
NATURAL FIRE AREA.

"Your travel through the fire area is an interesting opportunity
to observe Yellowstone in transition. Old forests and meadows
have burned and will rejuvenate, enhancing wildlife habitat."

And it looks a lot like an Irwin Allen disaster movie, too. Step
right up, folks.

That August there was talk of heads rolling over the let-burn
policy, but now, in retrospect, the idea that fire is needed to
maintain the overall health of the environment is officially seen
as "sound." Studies indicate that virtually everything is coming
back green, healthy, and vigorous and the fisheries don't seem to
have been affected one way or the other.

At this writing the fire policy in Yellowstone is still under
review—this is the government, after all, and these things take
time—but most park officials either hope or assume that some
natural fires will still be allowed to burn.

The Park Service said it expected the usual raft of tourists in
the summer of '89, plus a large contingent of the morbidly
curious, and that came to pass. With 2.6 million visitors to the
park, '89 was a record year. A friend of mine signed on as a fire
information officer to help handle the crowds.

I'll admit that, while in the thick of it, I occasionally got a little
freaked along with everyone else, even with my mystical/bio-
logically defensible outlook. Smoke, helicopters, and slurry
bombers filled the air, lines of tourists were leaving like
refugees, and I wasn't catching many trout. It was not a disaster
in any sense of the word, but it looked like one, and the press
was treating it like one. That kind of thing can embed itself in
your consciousness like a jingle for toothpaste, and be just as
hard to get rid of.

There was some serious excitement for a while, and some
tempers were clearly on edge, but now that the smoke has
cleared—as more than one clever reporter has put it—the powers
that be have assumed the attitude of a bored traffic cop after a
minor accident. "Okay, folks, move along, it's all over, nothing
more to see."

—

We broke out of our slump north of the park, near Livingston, Montana, when we bought a day on a private spring creek. The weather was hot, bright, and breezy, and the tab for the four of us was $120, but the spring water in the creek was wonderfully cold, and trout were rising lazily to Pale Morning Dun spinners when we drove over the wood bridge on the way to our assigned beat. We stopped both trucks to look as if we'd never seen anything like that before.

The wind was blowing out of the north, so, for once, there was no smoke in the air. None of that stink that's more like burning telephone poles than a campfire, and the sky was just plain blue.

Later that morning there was a long, steady hatch of duns, and by late afternoon the mayflies were back on the water a second time. The rainbow and brown trout fed on the flies in that prissy way they have in spring creeks, but they would go for a no-hackle or a parachute often enough that we were "catching fish" rather than "getting one now and then."

If you're not a fisherman, I can't begin to explain the importance of that distinction.

The current in the creek was slow and braided. The little yellow mayflies perched on the water and rode it downstream until they sailed into the air or were summarily eaten. Trout held in all the right spots, their rises sounding like small, hard objects being dropped into the water.

I'd gotten sloppy over the past days, and managed to break the fly off in the first fish I hooked. But I landed the next couple, and suddenly I was wired. It's funny how quickly it all comes back.

The creek appeared to go dead for a few hours in the early afternoon, as all creeks seem to do in the summer, but the wind was up, it was hot, and there we were in the middle of hayfields in August.

Grasshoppers, right?

There were none on the water, there were none in the

bankside grass. In fact, I hadn't seen a hopper anywhere in days, but this was a trout stream, and it was something that should work.

By the time the second mayfly hatch came on, I'd landed half a dozen fish—almost too easily—on a size 8 Henry's Fork Hopper that I'd bought back in Idaho. They were hefty trout that had chased and slashed the fly like dumb, small-stream brookies, with none of that snooty spring-creek reserve.

Maybe no one had ever thought to try a hopper here before. Or maybe I was just one sharp son of a bitch.

You know how it is.

As we were unstringing the rods at dark, A.K. produced the leather reel bag labeled "#5 line" which contains the pint of Canadian Club. By way of a toast, someone said, "Now that's the way it's *supposed* to be," and we drank to that.

It stuck in my mind, and I went to sleep that night on what seemed to be a fair question: how *is* it supposed to be?

That was the night A.K. started snoring and wouldn't stop, even after I'd rolled him over a few times trying different angles. So I took my sleeping bag out to the west side of the little cabin we'd rented (for shade in the morning) climbed in, thought, "Okay, how is . . . ?" and sailed into the finest night's sleep I'd had in weeks.

I woke to the smell of coffee and finished the thought. "It's supposed to be exactly as it is, however that happens to be at the moment."

It seemed profound as hell right then, but I didn't have time to even mention it to the boys because we were off in a big, excited hurry for the Lamar River and its rainbow/cutthroat hybrid trout. Normally you wouldn't want to fish the Lamar in August because the mosquitoes and black flies would be unbearable, and because it muddies up if a thundershower is even predicted. But this year was different. This year the wet meadows that breed the biting bugs had dried up because of the drought, and rain wasn't even a slight possibility.

What luck.

CHAPTER 9

NEITHER SNOW, NOR RAIN, NOR GLOOM OF NIGHT . . .

A.K. and I were camped on Roy Palm's place, with the tent pitched on a flat, grassy spot about halfway between his house and his stretch of the Frying Pan River. Roy had recently cleaned things up, so there was a big bulldozed pile of brush and tree limbs nearby that we were raiding nightly for firewood. After the first day, Roy's three retrievers, Tucker, Teal, and Rowly, had moved in with us. They'd be waiting predictably at the tent when we got back from fishing the evening rise. We liked the dogs' company and didn't mind the extra warmth at night either. This was a cold camp in late October.

It wasn't the last fishing trip of the year, but it was late enough that this was probably the last camp. So, largely to celebrate that, one night I handed A.K. the fresh pint of Southern Comfort I had stashed in my flytying kit. Sensing the gravity of the occasion, he removed the lid, tossed it into the fire, and we settled down to get ripped.

We do this once or twice a season and, although it's not as socially acceptable as it once was, I still feel it's perfectly all right. If you tend toward the urge to get in the pickup and drive to town looking for a fight, you shouldn't get drunk. But if, in the tradition of the sporting gentleman, you poke the fire, theorize, simplify, rant, preach, confess, and fall asleep, then you should if you want to.

The occasional peaceful bender in a solitary fishing camp is therapeutic, and I won't apologize for it. With the fresh air, cold water, and exercise, the hangovers aren't even too bad.

The confessions usually start about the time the Southern Comfort level has sunk below the riverboat on the label, and it never ceases to amaze me what a long and complicated past your average human being carries around. A.K. and I don't exactly "interface emotionally" or "share our feelings." In fact, we both tend to hold the midwestern stoic view that genuine problems are solved with action, not pissing and moaning. If you run around sharing your feelings too much, you'll eventually arrive at a place where you're not only still screwed up, but now everyone knows about it, too.

What A.K. and I do is just talk. We've been doing this for quite a while, and we now know things about each other that are none of *our* business, let alone yours.

It progressed, as it usually does on this high country river, to the point where we were sprawled next to the fire gazing at the stars, talking about how someday we should learn a little astronomy. Above the Frying Pan at night are the clearest sky and the brightest, most tightly packed stars I've ever seen, and I've been considerably higher.

In altitude, that is.

It was right after A.K. observed that a watched pot *does* boil, it just takes awhile, that I noticed the three faint dots next to the big star to the right of the moon. They were there in peripheral vision, but not straight on. I figured it was a mild hallucination, but when I mentioned it anyway, A.K. lurched to his feet and went to get the binoculars.

We learned later that this was Jupiter and three of its moons, an astonishingly rare sight to see with nothing but field glasses. This was one of the things Galileo saw through his telescope that led him to say publicly that those lights in the sky weren't holes poked in the roof by God, but other worlds. That got him in a lot of trouble with the Church, but he was still right.

At the time, we only knew it was a bad sign to be able to see something out in the universe that clearly from the bank of a trout stream. We'd come for the last of the Blue-winged Olive hatch, and what we'd hoped for was a falling barometer, low ceiling, and some wet, cold misery because that's when the Olive hatches are at their best.

Instead we'd had day after day of blue sky and sun, and night after night of stars. Colorado Indian summer. We'd caught some trout in the late afternoons by sheer persistence and it had been good—not to mention comfortable—but we were hoping for the hardship of cosmic weather and a great hatch to spice up the last of the season. There were good reasons why we both should have gotten back home to take care of some things, but we'd stayed on trying to wait out this disgustingly beautiful weather.

A brilliantly clear sky for three or four nights in a row meant stalled high pressure. It was beautiful—we aren't so gung ho that we're immune to that—but it did not bode well for the fishing.

The night of Jupiter's moons we almost went to sleep on the sobering thought that the weather was going to stay nice—and we couldn't just camp there waiting it out forever. But A.K., hopeful and drunk, pointed out that there would be more fishing yet this season; that if we were just patient we'd get dumped upon and frozen sooner or later.

Comforted by that, we shooed the dogs off our sleeping bags and turned in.

———

Weather is the key to fly-fishing. Foul weather, usually: imitation commando wool sweaters, hooded rain slickers, wool hats, fingerless gloves, long johns, wet cameras, wet camps, cold food, shots of whiskey for the illusion of warmth. It seems to have some weird connection to that good old Protestant ethic wherein anything that's easy or that feels good is sinful. You can catch trout on a warm, pretty day, of course, but you'll probably catch more if you suffer. In a strange, masochistic way, it only seems right.

Blue-winged Olives are the epitome of this. They're the only mayflies I'm familiar with that hatch predictably at least twice a year, in the spring and fall. Around here that's April and again in October, or maybe March and November in an unusual season. Whatever, the weather is likely to be dismal, and the bugs seem to love it. So much so that a sunny day can actually put a hatch off, although in practice nice weather is more likely to just reduce the duration and the number of bugs. There will be fishing, and it will be perfectly okay, but it's not the *great* fishing.

Ideal Blue-winged Olive weather is the kind that comes with the large, symmetrical movements of the big spring and fall storms. In April it may well be the first dump that's rain instead of snow, in October it's likely to be the other way around. Either way it will be damp, chilly, overcast, and generally grim.

At first there will be wind as the low pressure moves in. If you're on the river you'll probably fish, but the wind chill will ice up the guides on your rod and sandpaper your face and hands. A little of that goes a long way.

With luck, the front will move in and sit, the wind will die, and a thin drizzle will fall straight down, just heavily enough to take the sheen off the surface of the water. Then the mayflies hatch, typically in the late afternoon, and the trout rise up to eat them. This is not sporadic feeding, this is the main event.

A good Olive hatch exhibits one of those neat fits you now and then see in nature and sport. The bugs prefer to hatch in the same nasty weather that makes their wings dry slowly, which keeps them on the water and available to the trout longer. The trout, normally shy of bright light, seem to be more confident about rising to the surface on a dark, overcast day. It's carnage, but since our sympathies are with the fish it's also pretty.

And there you are. You're wet, you're miserable, you're catching trout, the stream isn't crowded, and you feel as if this is some kind of secret thing, as if this is what really happens out here when no one is around.

—

Accepted fly-fishing lore says the size 16 or 18 Blue-winged Olive that appears twice or sometimes three times a year is probably a Baetis, a small mayfly that produces multiple broods. The *little* Olive—about a size 22—is probably a Pseudocloeon.

Probably, I said.

Some of us use the Latin in the interest of entomological accuracy—not to mention showing off—but we still manage to turn it into a kind of slang. If you consult even a popular entomology book, you'll find that the #22 Blue-winged Olive could be a Pseudocloeon, Cloeon, or Neocloeon—probably one of the ten "more important" of these species, but not necessarily. The same kind of thing is true of the Baetis. In *Hatches* by Caucci and Nastasi, the authors point out that there are twenty different mayflies known as Blue-winged Olives.

To the authors' credit, they leave it to the reader to decide if this makes any difference.

I hold that it doesn't. In the field you fish the same patterns, in different sizes, on a long, light tippet and a dead drift, preferably in the rain.

The insect itself looks delicate to some, but I see it as compact and sturdy, like a Jack Russell terrier. Little, yes, but anything but fragile. The bugs' coloring is dull, chilly-looking, and vaguely military: a cross between faded olive drab and battleship gray. In the air, a Blue-winged Olive vanishes as soon as he's above the trees and against the gray sky. I think his coloration is weather-specific camouflage, although I can't cite chapter and verse for that. It's my own idea. A bug that hatches on gray days and stands a good chance of being eaten by a trout before he can get airborne would be wise to be gray himself on the off chance that it might make a slight difference.

—

Foul weather. The worst A.K. and I ever fish in on purpose is
in January and February. This is accomplished with a fly rod in
flowing water, but I don't see it as entirely real fishing. That is,
if it were all like this, I might consider changing sports. It's just
that a few rivers are open, the season here doesn't close, and so
it can be done. It's a haunting possibility in a part of the season
that seems to demand celebration.

After all, the arrival of the new year is the fisherman's holiday.
Not Christmas. Christmas—even in the crass way it's observed
now—is still a necessarily public display for family and society,
and every real fisherman is essentially an anarchist. He may be
faithful and law-abiding, but he still views those entanglements
with some justifiable suspicion. He wants to be out when
everyone else is in. Eventually I think he comes to crave
loneliness.

A "real" fisherman is one who thinks like I do. There are more
of us around than you might suspect.

The fisherman feels more comfortable with New Year's
because, even though it misses the actual winter solstice by
more than a week when placed at January 1, it is still essentially
astronomical in nature, and has the flavor about it of a great,
cyclic movement so silent and portentous you could miss it
altogether if some TV weatherman didn't point out the longest
night of the year.

Also, the need for a new fishing license surfaces, and one cold
morning, you realize that you have not caught a single fish "this
year."

Sometime before Christmas I go over to Ted's Hardware to
get a brand-new, unwrinkled, resident small game hunting and
fishing license. It's made of a wonderful kind of thin, silky,
waterproof paper that won't tear. Flytier John Betts makes wings
for caddis flies out of the same stuff.

I buy the license early so I won't forget later, and so there
won't be a single minute when I couldn't be afield and legal with
a rod or gun if I felt like it. I like to get the very first license from
the very first book—numero uno—because I think it must be
lucky, but usually someone beats me to it. I once thought about

having Ted save it for me, but you can't cheat luck. It might appear to work at the moment, but later it will turn on you in some particularly spooky way, and it's best not to mess with that. Also, Ted might think I was getting strange on him, and how one is viewed at the hardware store is not inconsequential around here.

Then, come New Year's Eve, I'll tip one to the instant when last year's license expires and this year's kicks in. This is symbolic of the actual new year: that moment when the sun appears to freeze in the sky over the Tropic of Capricorn, and then starts plodding its way north again. That's the kind of subtle event a fisherman can get his teeth into.

Then, sometime in the first weeks of the fresh year, A.K. and I go out and try to catch a couple of trout. We do this as though it were an observance.

The first trout of the year: it *seems* as if it should mean something, so we try to accomplish the feat with bamboo rods, in a river, with flies. Preferably dry flies. For some reason that I'd be hard pressed to explain rationally, a nymph is okay, but ice fishing doesn't count.

Usually by the time this rolls around there has been very little, if any, fishing for a couple of months. September, of course, was glorious—typically the best dry fly fishing of the year; October held on for a couple of weeks, but the high-altitude lakes and streams were off from the cold, if not actually frozen over, and the ones down lower were getting moody.

The Blue-winged Olives happened at least once, either on the Frying Pan or the South Platte: a dank, hideous day of wild fishing at the end of which we wring out clothing, drive to a bar, and sit in a corner steaming, sipping coffee, looking mean and crazy.

Fishermen openly enjoy being thought of as crazy.

And there was the hunting. Deer, maybe a trip for upland birds, and rabbits, which are my favorites because they're so much like trout. The bunny season is long; the hunting casual; you can use something like a Ted Hatfield small-bore flintlock rifle—the firearm equivalent of a bamboo fly rod; and there are days when you get some and days when you don't. Mostly it's that: the lack of pressure when compared to big game. No one ever comes over to your table at the café to ask, "Get your rabbit yet?"

By this time A.K. has gotten pretty easy to find. He has settled into his basement shop to mass-produce flies. More and more these days, they're big-ticket tarpon and billfish patterns. The radio is tuned to a jazz station, the perpetual coffeepot is on, the perpetual pipe is smoldering, and he's going through feathers at about the same rate as if he were manufacturing pillows.

And I more or less settle into my own office to write, although my weekly outdoor page at the newspaper forces me out now and then so I'll have something to write *about*. The old "I remember what my daddy taught me when I was nine years old" stuff fills in gaps in the winter, but it soon wears thin.

This is not bad at all, especially in cold weather. A long time ago Charles Waterman said that writing about the outdoor sports gets to be more fun than actually doing them. Well, not always, but I see now that he's basically correct.

It was also awhile ago that Nick Lyons said it's good for the soul to have a closed season on fishing. Same idea, different angle. Not fishing for a while gives you a perspective on the sport that being in the thick of it never will. You remember things—good, solid, revealing things—that might otherwise have drifted on downstream and gone out of sight forever.

More recently, Nick wrote from New York to say he still believes that, but added, "The closed part doesn't have to be *so* long, does it?"

Colorado once had a closed season, but no more. Now you can fish any day of the year you can stand to be out. I don't know why that is, and I've never asked. It seems like such a reasonable, tolerant, hands-off sort of policy that it may have been a mistake, and I'd hate to inadvertently call it to anyone's attention.

So it's the new year, easily two and a half to three months till the beginnings of the thaw, but still—by the grace of the powers that be—time to catch the first trout.

This can seem unlikely. By January there is usually snow on the ground even at the lower altitudes, and in the mountains you need skis or snowshoes to get around. It's cold. It's around then that my plumbing typically freezes up, along with the pipes in a number of other old houses along the north, south, and main branches of the creek where, on clear nights, the coldest air settles like doom. I find myself thinking, This is water—the same stuff trout live in—and I can't even get it from the well to the kitchen faucet, let alone the extra eighteen feet to the bathroom.

But then I walk over to the creek to fetch the water that will let me flush the pot. The Island Pool is frozen bank to bank, but below it there's enough open current to dip the bucket into. And this is just a freestone stream, in low flow and unfishable now. The tailwaters will be open, and trout will be feeding. I can picture it. All we need is a day when the air temperature is high enough to keep the line from freezing in the guides.

The thing is, it's easy to pass on winter fishing. You have to summon a little basic courage to do it. You'll be cold, and your pack will be heavy from all the survival junk you'd be stupid not to bring along. But you have to do it because not doing it means you've gotten tired or lazy or too busy, all of which are bad signs.

Once you're past the inertia, a kind of optimism takes over. The odds are against it, but it might be great. It's been great in the past. And, good or bad, it will be exclusive, even on a river that's usually crowded. You think, Any idiot can fish in the summer.

A.K. and I begin turning to the weather maps in our morning newspapers where we pay special attention to the coasts of Oregon and Washington that get first what we usually get a few days later. And we watch the five-day forecasts on the tube, the ones with the adorable little smiling suns and frowning clouds. These are presided over by painfully clean-cut announcers who make the now-common assumption that getting to work on time, and to the ski slopes on the weekends, is the moral goal of the universe, and that the respiration of the planet where we all evolved is just a periodic inconvenience.

We don't want the bright winter thaw, we want the *end* of the
thaw, the day when the barometer starts to drop and the sky gets
ash-colored. Even if nothing else happens, the fishing can be
good. Often it only involves drifting tiny midge larva flies
painstakingly on the bottoms of the deepest pools and getting
the odd, lazy strike. Sometimes there'll be a decent midge hatch
and we can fish little dry flies. And sometimes there will be
the elusive third Blue-winged Olive hatch that I've never
seen on a freestone stream, but have occasionally stumbled upon
on tailwaters. Until the moment I see them I think mayflies
would be as unlikely in the middle of winter as butterflies or
mosquitoes.

That's the gamble on timing.

We do it every year, because sooner or later there's the day
that comes every few seasons when we drive to the river on a
gloomy, threatening morning and land thirty trout on dry flies,
just like that.

We hike out in a bitter wind and drive slowly back home in the
blizzard to arrive home very late. Wives and girlfriends have seen
the snow, have heard the travelers' advisories, and have worried
enough that they're mad when we finally get in. No motherly
smiles. We are idiots, they say. Later, when it becomes obvious
that we're not even sorry, we may become reckless, thoughtless
bastards.

We're not sorry because the beauty of this kind of fishing is
found exactly in its unpleasantness and its appearance of risk. It
leaves you tired and a little distant.

———

It was in April of last year that A.K. and I decided to tumble
for all the publicity and drive over to Utah to fish the famous
Green River. A few days before we left I called our guide,
Dennis Breer, and learned that the Blue-winged Olives were
hatching nicely. When I called A.K. to tell him that, he said,
"Did you hear the weather report? They say it's going to be
'unsettled.'"

That's what it was. The first afternoon, after checking in with Dennis and setting the tent up in a nearby campground that, miraculously, still had some usable firewood lying around in it, we put in a couple of hours right below the dam, mostly within sight of the paved boat ramp. It had been a lukewarm, sunny day, but the light went off the water early down in the canyon, and as soon as that happened the trout started hitting. We caught some. Not a lot, but plenty for the first two hours on a brand-new river.

The next day we floated from the dam to Little Hole, and the day after that from Little Hole down to Indian Crossing. For the first float the canyon is steep, sparsely wooded in ponderosa and juniper, and the rocks are brilliantly red: the Flaming Gorge. Down lower it opens up a bit, shades from iron oxide red to a more sandy color, and there are sage and yucca on the hillsides. Somewhere in there it goes from mostly rainbows and cutthroats to mostly *browns* and cutthroats—an unusual mix of fish that made the river seem more exotic.

There was a high patchy overcast in the sky above much of the trip, the cool beginnings of a large, slow-moving front coming in from the northwest. Sometimes it would clear and get warm enough to shed a sweater, sometimes it would drizzle enough to require a slicker. Twice there was enough rain and lightning to drive us off the water into the shelter of the cliffs. The fishing came and went in classic response to the weather: the nastier it was the better it was.

It was on the Green that I made what was, for me, at least, a new observation. I knew that Blue-winged Olives seem to like to hatch in the afternoons, but it had never before occurred to me that it's also in the afternoons that the storms build. I would prefer not to believe that this is just a coincidence.

———

Over the years I've asked a number of fisheries biologists about the connection between weather and fishing. I've learned surprisingly little, but here it is:

All freshwater game fish are photosensitive to some degree, preferring low light to bright, direct sunlight. There may be some genetic predisposition to this, but it's probably learned behavior for the most part. Bright light means exposure to predators, while darkness or shade means safety. In some extreme cases—like brown trout or largemouth bass living in heavily fished waters—the fish can become entirely nocturnal.

Low light in the daytime comes from deep water, shady banks, structures like bridges and docks, and, best of all, lousy weather.

Rain, drizzle, sleet, snow, and wind accomplish the same thing: they texture the surface of the water, lowering visibility, and making the fish feel safer.

Of course it's not quite that simple. Too much rain or snow at the wrong time of year can lower the water temperature and put the fish off. Most of the trouts become sluggish and pouty in water that gets below about 45 degrees. It's entirely possible to have too much of a good thing, especially early and late in the season.

Fine, that part of it makes perfect sense. Fish, especially trout, like crappy weather for largely understandable reasons, but fisherpeople have this mystical streak that searches for deeper meanings and hidden connections.

The barometer is a kind of icon to some fishermen. Given a choice, they'll sit home when it's high and call in sick to work when it starts to fall. The scientists have told me that trout do have sensitive lateral lines that doubtless perceive subtle changes in pressure—and it's known that air pushes on water. Okay, but they say that a trout swimming from two feet of water to three feet experiences a much greater change in pressure than he'd feel from the wildest imaginable change in the holy barometer. It's not the barometer at all, they say, it's the gray sky, wind, drizzle, and such that comes with low pressure. The barometer business is probably nothing but an old husbands' tale, they tell me.

I guess I don't believe that, especially since I could swear I've seen trout begin to feed furiously *as* the barometer was dropping, and *before* the sky clouded up or the rain started to fall. I can't shake the feeling that they know.

Look at it this way. We humans, especially those who live in cities, are constantly victimized by sudden and vast changes in everything from noise levels to the particulate content of the air, but we still somehow manage to react radically to the subtlest of signals, like a passing whiff of a familiar perfume or an offhand comment in a peaceful conversation that might just have been an insult.

A pair of fishermen camped along a trout stream might even decide to get shit-faced on a clear night because they feel instinctively that tomorrow's fishing will be a little slow, so a hangover won't hurt anything.

More than once it's occurred to me that I should stop talking to scientists if I'm not going to believe what they tell me.

We caught a lot of trout in two days of floating the Green with Dennis, and we found him to be a fine, mellow guide. Even that early in the season the river was a little crowded with boats, but when we'd come to a jam we'd either pull over and let everyone else go by, or row on down to some fresh water. "Plenty of river here," Dennis would say. "Plenty of fish for everyone."

We fished Blue-winged Olive dries and emergers during the afternoon hatches, and nymphs and streamers to fill in the blanks. The weather was better than it could have been, but it was still bad enough for good fishing, and we never got so cold that we had to beach the mackenzie boat and start a fire, never got so wet that our clothes didn't pretty much dry out overnight.

When we pulled in at the take-out spot on the evening of the second day, it had begun to rain lightly. By morning the canyon was socked in with one of those wet, cold, smoky-looking western storms that sift clouds down into the tops of the trees. The weather map in the local newspaper showed the front sliding gradually east into Colorado, just beginning to swallow up the Frying Pan River.

We broke camp and stopped to tell Dennis we were heading
for the Pan. He couldn't understand it. "Fish here," he said,
"it'll be great. You can hike down the canyon and wade. Why
drive all the way over there?"

It was hard to explain. We had caught lots of trout, including
some real big ones, and had seen roughly sixteen miles of
gorgeous western river canyon from the luxurious vantage point
of a slow-drifting, old-style wooden mack boat. There were
wondrous things yet to see: more river on downstream where,
rumor had it, fewer fishermen went and the browns were even
bigger. Later there might be a hatch of acacia bugs or a migration
of strange Mormon crickets that would run across the surface of
the river and die by the thousands in the mouths of huge trout.

You have to be careful of greed on a good, new river. You can
beat yourself up and finally limp away still without having had
enough.

And then there was this weather, a flat, wet, low-pressure
storm stalled there on the Green, but also over a familiar river six
hours south and east. When it looks as if it's going to be
absolutely, horribly wonderful, you want to be on water you
know so you can take full advantage of it.

As I said, I don't think Dennis ever quite understood. Maybe
he thought we were scared to stay and fish in the rain.

———

We called ahead and Roy said we could camp on his place
again if we wanted to. It was raining when we got there. The
dogs were glad to see us, but they were also wet, so we wouldn't
let them in the tent. They slunk back to the barn, puzzled and
offended, still carrying the sticks they'd expected us to throw for
them.

Some other fly-fishermen were on to this, too, but there
weren't crowds of them, as there often are on the Pan in more
hospitable weather. A few other fishermen are okay. In fact,
when you're out there suffering together, a nice feeling of
camaraderie develops. You wave at each other, stop to talk more

freely. No one actually says it, but you all feel as if you're among the precious few who know how it is and aren't being wimps about it.

We started fishing in the flats below the dam where the big rainbows are known to lie. This is the top end of the catch-and-release area, a spot that, at many times of the year, is too packed with fishermen to even bother with. There were two guys downstream at the bend pool, and one above carefully working the bank. Before the day was out we would run up there to watch him land a nine-pound rainbow.

Plenty of river, plenty of fish for everyone.

The trout were supposed to be eating shrimp then, and shrimp patterns worked. Not beautifully—hardly anything works "beautifully" in an established catch-and-release area—but the right-sized fly drifted in the right way through the perfect spot would draw a strike. It might take fifteen or twenty casts and two fly changes to a fish you could see. If you couldn't see the fish, but believed one was there, it could take longer.

That afternoon we each landed a couple of the square, chunky rainbows the Pan has gotten famous for in recent years. These fish are big, but not pretty. They resemble slabs of bacon, and that's how some of them fight, too, but they're impressive as hell, all the more so for being so ugly.

They're not easy to land either. These fish fight with their weight, which is considerable, and that is often enough. I hooked one that ran me a good hundred yards downstream, right past the two fishermen down there. The fish gained line on me the whole way and broke off as he went around the bend.

"Probably foul hooked," one of the guys said, which was meant as either sour grapes or consolation, I couldn't tell which.

"Yeah, probably," I said.

I didn't take many photos for fear of drowning a perfectly good Pentax K-1000, but I have one from that first afternoon of A.K. holding his big landing net out toward the camera with a trout in it so big the head sticks out on one side and the tail flops out on the other. He's wearing so many layers of wool and chamois that his rain slicker looks like a sausage. His hood is pulled almost closed, leaving just enough room for him to see out and to get the pipe into his mouth. You can just see the top row of teeth from what must be a dazed grin. Apparently it wasn't raining too hard at the moment because he has the pipe upright and it still seems to be lit.

The first night was wet and cold. We stayed in our waders and slickers to cook supper, and then ate in the tent. It was too nasty for evening fire sitting, too wet for a fire, and there was no wood anyway. Roy had done something with the brush pile.

The following day we caught more big fish, and that night we huddled in the tent discussing possible designs for a tarp arrangement off the back of the camper shell on the pickup that would let us cook out of the rain. We also noted that the tent was taking on a little water.

On the morning of the third day we drove into Basalt for breakfast at the café rather than face the dripping camp kitchen. This is a trout town, so they know what fishermen are. There were no weird looks, and no unnecessary conversation either. Waitresses in Basalt know that fishermen who look as bad as we did are best left to mutter among themselves.

Breakfast was reviving—pancakes, sausages, lots of coffee— and we set out on what had become the daily schedule only an hour or so late. First to the flats to nymph for hogs, then a lunch break in the steaming cab of the truck with soggy sandwiches and thermos coffee, then to the stretch above the Picnic Hole for the Blue-winged Olive hatch.

The day was hours old before either of us noticed that we were alone. An empty river in a storm is sublime enough; when it's one that is normally crowded it also has some of the poignancy of a deserted city street on a November morning.

A.K. was working the long run just below the concrete bridge, and I was above it, casting to rising trout in the big pool there. The mayflies were coming off well, and fish were lined up, rising steadily and in a quick, efficient rhythm. It was almost easy.

A pelting rain was falling, giving the river a rough slate finish that the trout could just see the bugs through. It was lovely. Fishermen can get nearly religious about the texture of water. There were lots of mayflies, and very few bugs were getting off the surface. Many were, in fact, smashed flat and nearly drowned. I was fishing a damp no-hackle dun that was floating on its side just like the naturals. The fish loved it.

I'd landed half a dozen good rainbows—and I knew A.K. had done about the same downstream, judging from the muffled whooping I'd heard from that direction—when I saw the big head coming up over near the far bank. This was a very large fish, lying in a large fish spot: a willow-lined eddy where the stream flows backward for ten or fifteen feet. He seemed to be standing on his tail, bobbing up to take a mayfly every four or five seconds.

I caught him. I simply crossed over the bridge, found a good casting position, made a single decent cast, and hooked the fish. He bored for the bottom a few times, and when he went for the main current I had just enough of my wits about me to splash out there (nearly going in) and pull on him in the exact direction he wanted to go. Feeling that pressure, he instinctively swam against it, as any of *us* would do in a moment of panic, and turned back into the slow water where I was able to land him. I'll say he was a thick twenty-four or -five inches and an honest five pounds.

Yes, it was a brilliant job of fish playing. Thank you very much.

The clouds were low enough that I couldn't see the lip of the canyon, only where the red cliffs, now more of an antique rust color, dissolved. The rocks were wet and shiny, with rainwater running over them, sometimes in flat sheets, sometimes in little eroding streams that you could somehow hear over the noise of the rain and the river. The stream itself made the usual slurping sound of current with overtones of the rain sizzling on its surface. Now and then a rock would come loose and fall with a clacking sound. All this had the effect of silence.

I was wet to the skin, wearing as much of my second change of clothing as I could get on. Later, in a warmer, friendlier place,

I would find that my body was as pale and wrinkled as a dead fish. When I sat down on the bank and leaned against a rock, I squished inside the rubber suit. I felt cold. I felt as if I had perhaps gone slightly mad. I felt as if I'd just discovered North America and wasn't going to tell anyone about it.

A.K. came crashing down to the stream through the willows and said, "The hatch is over, let's go sit in the truck and warm up." It sounded like a very sane suggestion.

There had been no other fishermen, and all day only two or three cars had passed on the road, but as we climbed out of the river a guy in some kind of a sports car pulled up. He rolled his window down two inches and said through the crack, "Getting any big fish."

"I just landed a five-pound rainbow on a number eighteen dry fly," I said.

"No no," he said, "I mean *really big* fish."

The guy was young, well dressed, dry, warm, and sitting in a sports car with the heater going.

"You're an asshole," I said.

A.K. agreed. Only an asshole would insult a wet fisherman's trout.

It seemed over, so we drove slowly back to camp. On the outside the tent was sagging pitifully. Inside our sleeping bags and pads were floating in four inches of standing rainwater. The air had cooled enough that our breath was condensing into thin clouds.

The dogs had run out when we pulled in and were now standing there watching us expectantly. Suddenly I couldn't remember how many days we'd been out. Seven maybe.

"A.K.," I said, "I think I wanna go home."

cHApTER 10

Fly-fishing's National Bird

 Naturally, my friend Gil began referring to me as "the poultry king of northern Colorado" even before the chicks arrived from the hatchery in Iowa City. It had only been a year since I'd bought the place on the creek and become the lord and master of a sprawling quarter acre of river bottom, complete with an aging, poorly insulated house. There'd been some things to do, but eventually the first roof patch was completed, the wood stove was installed, several cords of firewood were in, and the garden was planted. The next step, before building the smokehouse, was to start raising some chickens.

Ah, but not just any chickens. These birds were going to supply meat, eggs, and, perhaps most importantly, flytying materials. I was going to heat with wood—which I'd cut myself in the National Forest—eat home-grown eggs, fried chicken, and vegetables, hunt, fish with flies tied with feathers from my own birds, and otherwise be as self-sufficient as possible.

I wasn't exactly working from a manifesto, but it was clear to my friends what I was up to. When Ed Engle arrived to check out the new place, he found me splitting pine logs for the stove and said, "Well, isn't this just organic as hell?"

Well, yes, that was the general idea.

There were also two or three cats, a half-crazy, deeply territorial dalmatian, and Carol. That was over a dozen years ago. One of the cats, the dog, the girl, and all the chickens are no longer around. Let's talk about the chickens.

The first question was, what breed? Blue Andalusians sprang to mind for their blue dun hackles, the most coveted and hardest to find, and so, by implication, the classiest. Face it, fly-fishing is a classy sport—even the blue-collar branch of it. I could easily picture a couple of Blue Andalusian roosters strutting imperially around the place: Blue-winged Olives on the hoof.

When tied properly, the hackle for that fly is natural blue dun (as opposed to dyed), and the wings are made from a pair of round, webby cape feathers from an Andalusian hen. There'd be six or eight of those sitting in the chicken coop growing hackle for dry fly wings. Almost as an afterthought, they'd also be laying some eggs.

I could picture it, and as a picture it looked good, but the barest research showed me what a bad idea it was.

Apparently the coveted blue dun color on an Andalusian is recessive, so for every rooster you get of even roughly the right shade, you'll also get a whole mess of blacks and whites. And it must be kept in mind that a modest, working, egg-producing, chicken *re*producing barnyard flock is mostly hens, while, of course, the much-sought-after dry fly hackles come from the adult, two- or even three-year-old roosters. And this was supposed to be a small, funky operation: feathers for personal use only.

Translation: blue dun hackle meant too many birds, potentially too much waiting, and too much uncertainty. I had limited space, and limited patience, so whatever birds I got would have to be guaranteed usable, that is, predictably the right color, if nothing else.

The second logical choice was grizzly hackle, which comes from a handsome, hardy, brown egg-laying bird called a barred Plymouth Rock. The rooster hackle goes into dozens of useful dry flies, and the saddles—either natural or dyed—are used on at least as many streamers and bass bugs. Grizzly hackle for a fly tier is about as standard a material as pine lumber for a carpenter.

But most of all, grizzly is the prime material for the Adams: a grizzly hackle mixed with a brown for the collar, and griz hen for the wings. The Adams is America's favorite dry fly, which would make the barred rock fly-fishing's national bird.

A barred rock feather, if you've never seen one, is silvery white with a regular ladder-rung pattern in charcoal. As the wing on a streamer it makes a variegated pattern like the parr marks on a young trout, as wound hackle on a dry fly it seems to scatter and fuzz the light, making the fly look "buggy," whatever that means.

On the live bird you get an effect that's not quite striped or mottled, certainly not spotted like a dalmatian, although dalmatians and barred rocks do look like they're vaguely related.

Yes, a small flock of those would look just fine. In retrospect, I think the image was as important to me as the finished product.

Best of all, every last barred Plymouth Rock is *barred*. There would be no genetic crap games.

I made the half-ruined shed out back into something of a chicken coop by building nesting boxes, running in a light fixture, buying a feeder and a watering device, scattering some grass hay around, and cutting a chicken-sized (and also raccoon-sized) hatch at ground level that could be closed and latched every night.

Leslie M. Black, writing in *A Practical Guide to Successful Farming* (copyright, 1943), said, "Poultry keeping is basically a business of details." Sure, I could have gotten a newer book, but how much could this have changed in forty years?

I started small with a handful of chicks that were brought by UPS in something like a shoe box. I paid a little extra to have them "sexed," so I knew what I had: eight hens and two roosters.

Or one rooster too many.

Roosters fight, it turns out, not long after their combs begin to appear and they start learning to crow. Roosters fight because they firmly believe that they hold exclusive rights to any and all hens in the county. Based on that assumption, they are willing to kill, and they don't have survival considerations to distract them. Domestication has not made these birds noble. They tend to peck each other on the back of the neck, right in that valuable band of #14 and #16 hackle.

It's also a fallacy that roosters crow at sunrise. The fact is, they *begin* to crow at sunrise (or when the gas station next door turns on its lights, whichever comes first), and they keep at it pretty much all day long. With two of them you get both solos and harmony.

In the dead of winter when the nights get well below freezing, one way to keep the chicken coop heated a bit is to leave a light on in there, which naturally makes the roosters crow all night long. At three in the morning you can find yourself toying with the idea of turning the light out so they'll shut up. It might not even be a tragedy if they froze to death.

The hens, by comparison, were sweet, quiet, innocent things. Not animals you'd get attached to or name, but definitely unobtrusive. Of course it was the foul-tempered roosters I was really interested in.

For the most part, being a part-time amateur hackle raiser was like having a bum knee: you get used to it, but you never actually come to like it.

There was some satisfaction in the trips to the feed store, where I could suddenly qualify as some kind of farmer rather than just another hippie buying birdseed. I also enjoyed the toting of fifty-pound bags of chicken feed, which was nice and cheap. The eggs were big, brown-shelled, orange-yolked, and delicious. I ate some and sold just enough of them to a neighbor at a dollar a dozen to pay for the feed, which added a satisfying zero investment footnote to the whole operation.

I penned the birds up for a while, but mostly to keep the two roosters from fighting, I ended up just letting them run. They stayed together and didn't go far—if you really wanted to find them it wouldn't take more than ten minutes. Around dusk they always came back to the coop, and one of the daily details was to shut them inside for the night so the critters wouldn't get them.

Or, let's say, so the critters couldn't get them too easily. There were the inevitable casualties.

It turns out that an unsupervised flock of chickens, left to their own meager devices, will eat just about anything, including the garden if the gate is left open, but they do give a place a nice rustic ambience. The first time Gil saw loose chickens waddling around the place, he said, "Well, here we are in Dogpatch, Colorado."

Everyone should have a friend like Gil.

To this day I picture chickens when I hear the word "rural" and get a warm feeling when I see a place with these stupid but useful birds standing around on it. Chickens mean involved settlement. Yuppies living in the country don't have chickens, neither do extended families of bikers. Chickens are more common around houses that don't have satellite dishes in the yards.

Still, the hackle business didn't work out too well. I killed and skinned the first rooster at two years, just after Christmas. I'd been told the feathers would be at their best when the bird was in its winter plumage.

The hackles were . . . Well, let's be kind and say they were usable. Their shape was a little too short and wide, and there were no feathers on the neck small enough to tie a #18 dry fly—and precious few #16s, for that matter. Overall the quality was marginal, that is, as dry fly hackle, they were too soft.

I found I could make a passable size 12 or 14 Adams if I mixed my grizzly with a good, long Metz brown to take up the slack. In the interest of integrity, I used cottontail rabbit fur from a bunny I'd shot that winter for the body on those flies.

Okay, fine. That was all very pure and self-reliant, but I never could elude the fact that good flies are made from top-quality materials. I will say that, given the right stuff to work with, I can make pretty good trout flies.

It was that part of winter when spring becomes foreseeable, and so the serious flytying had started. I fought the idea, but after only a few sessions at the vise I had to admit that I'd taken two years to grow some fair-to-middling wet fly hackle and some marginal saddles: the kind of material you can pick up at the fly shop for pocket change.

By spring I'd used feathers from my bird to tie some decent streamers and wet flies. As I'd anticipated, catching a trout on a fly that you not only tied yourself, but for which you'd also raised some of the materials, was a kick.

Well, maybe "kick" is too strong a word.

That was the beginning of the end of the chicken ranching venture, and also an ancient lesson. I began to see that things like currency and commerce weren't invented just because people had nothing better to do. It was because some folks did certain things better than others (like raise hackle, for instance) and because total country subsistence often means just getting by: wearing the same shirt and eating the same meal every day, and even putting up with the indignity of fishing with ratty-looking dry flies.

It became obvious that tying the flies myself would have to be good enough. Better for me to write more stories so I could *buy* good hackle and get on with it. Let Metz and Hoffmann worry about which rooster to breed to which hen, and chase off raccoons and coyotes in the middle of the night, out there in the dark stark-naked juggling a flashlight and shotgun. Let *their* chickens sneak into the garden and eat all the snow peas.

———

I got into flytying after the most recent entomological phase had begun, but just before the current fashion for synthetic materials really began to take hold. There was a kind of engaging alchemy about materials then, and a good deal of hair splitting—if you'll pardon the pun.

For instance, for the dubbed body of an Adams dry fly you wanted to use not the gray underfur of a cottontail rabbit, but the gray underfur of a muskrat. The colors and consistencies of the two materials are almost exactly the same, but the rat is a water animal, you see, so his fur is naturally treated with moisture-resistant oils that aid in the flotation of the fly.

Well, maybe, maybe not. If it does make a difference, it would have to be a small one. The point is, it *sounded* right. That was enough for arcane types like fly-fishermen.

Now everyone knew that muskrat was supposed to be better than rabbit for gray-bodied dry flies, but there was another wrinkle. (There were always footnotes. It was great.)

Fly shop owners liked to deal with tanned hides because they weren't greasy, didn't stink, and weren't as likely to grow colonies of bugs. But the really savvy flytier knew that what you wanted was *untanned* muskrat because the tanning process removed the natural oils you were after in the first place.

So, if you were cool, you'd be able to show your friends a fragrant, salted, green muskrat hide you'd gotten from a trapper—possibly some local farm kid—for two dollars. You didn't need a prime hide because you were going to cut it up anyway.

This was the genuine article, and you'd have gotten off a lot cheaper than if you'd bought that much muskrat fur at the shop.

Better material, more of it for less money, and from an authentic source, too. Never mind that it smelled and bred vermin, you had entered into the upper reaches of materials procurement. God, you could be wise about that stuff.

I once heard an idle theory spun by a guy on a long drive to a river somewhere to the effect that a muskrat from a cold climate should have more oil in its fur than one from a warmer place, so it would probably float the fly better. This was just a fisherman killing time, but it had the ring of truth about it. If that idea had ever found its way into print, there would have been a discreet run among the informed on muskrats from the Yukon Territory.

Of course, now that we have good liquid fly flotants, you can use anything you want for dubbing and not worry about the subtleties. I suppose that's an improvement.

Still, there was a long and respected history behind this kind of thing, and if you entered the sport at the right time you imprinted on it. For instance, you aren't likely to find it in recently published books, but the original dressing for the Light Cahill dry fly calls for a dubbed body made from the naturally urine-burned red fox fur from the belly of a vixen. This isn't something you'd run into every day, nor would there be much of it on any one fox, but it was definitely The Right Stuff.

At one time the dubbing for a Tupps Indispensable was listed as the fine, glossy fuzz found in the neighborhood of a ram's testicles. Substitutes were offered later, but in the beginning a Tupps just wouldn't work without the correct material. It was, after all, "indispensable."

A tupp is a ram, by the way. You couldn't just say "ram." That would be too easily understood by the uninitiated.

The recipes for some of these old flies read like incantations. In the older books you'd only be slightly surprised to find a pattern calling for powdered bat wing. Not all materials were like this, but there was something magical about stuff that was weird, hard to find, possibly a little distasteful, and that came in small, precious amounts. I mean, how much fuzz could the average ram *have* on his balls, anyway?

Unlike what you hear now about flytying theory, this was not science. It was more like a naturalistic theology. Whatever color, texture, or effect you needed on a fly could be found ready-made in nature, as if it were put there for just that purpose as part of the original plan for the universe. Usually—conveniently—it was found in the furs and feathers of animals that were already hunted for food, trapped for pelts, or executed as varmints. A list of standard flytying materials reads like a journal from a good hunting season: deer hair and bucktail, elk, black bear, mallard, wood duck, teal, grouse, partridge, turkey, muskrat, fox, squirrel, rabbit, and so on.

There was even a time when fly patterns had a regional flavor based on the kind of game that was hunted where the flies were tied.

There were exceptions, of course, the major one being dry fly hackle that came from domestic roosters or from imported Indian gamecocks. Dry fly hackle does not grow wild in this country.

Still, there was this aura of self-sufficiency to it all. It was easy enough to develop an image of the flytier as all-around woodsman/folk artist who lived off the land, using everything but the bones and cobs: a guy with a fowling piece leaning in the corner and roosters strutting in the yard. Even in the old days, maybe one in a hundred was like that, and he probably wasn't a professional. But then myths and fishing stories have to do with the exceptional rather than the everyday.

It's because of that image that I like natural materials. In the right mood I can even get pretty mystical about something like shooting a Hungarian partridge, eating partridge paprika for supper—possibly with a decent bottle of wine and a very close friend—and then tying soft hackled wet flies with the beautiful brown mottled flank feathers. If nothing else, it's a better than average excuse—if one was needed—to go bird hunting.

Naturally, you should choose this friend carefully, especially if it's a woman, because she, like a lot of people, may just not *get* the hunting business. You'll want to do this anyway in the interest of the quality of the conversation. I've found that people who are squeamish about game are often the same ones who lack an appreciation of subtlety in other areas as well.

No, they're not all women, though many of them are.

You love the things you shoot; you kill and eat the things you love, and feel proud to have game on the table without entirely forgetting the remorse you felt when you dropped it. Then you tie flies with some of what's left over which you use to catch fish, which you also claim to love. A few of these you kill, most you release.

This is sport. Take it from me, it is a lofty and philosophical pursuit.

Still, for some people there are too many nuances there. They'd feel a lot more comfortable if you killed birds because you hated them.

———

One of the sweetest things about natural furs and feathers is that they vary. Synthetics don't. When I tie green damselfly nymphs I make the body from #3 FLY-RITE, a synthetic that's exactly the color I want and that's very easy to work with. The only thing wrong with it is, it's absolutely uniform. When I go down to the fly shop to get a package of the stuff, there's no need for me to paw through all of them, no chance I'll get a bad one or an especially good one.

For that matter, there's also no chance that I'll bag one during the FLY-RITE season and get a whole skin for nothing. No opportunity to say, as I sometimes *can* say of deer, rabbit, squirrel, partridge, and grouse, "Some people buy their FLY-RITE, but I, of course, shoot my own."

On the other hand, when I go to pick out a rooster neck, I can spend two hours examining each one for hackle length, size, color, sheen, web, and stiffness of barbule. Maybe I get the best one and maybe I don't, but I sure get the one I want.

The process can look pretty impressive, too. There are a few people around here who think I really know my rooster necks because I used to raise them.

———

There are lots of synthetic materials in use now—most marketed with the same kind of claims you'll hear for dishwashing detergent—and sometimes I worry that, what with graphite and boron rods, plastic lines, monofilament leaders, neoprene waders, and flies tied with petrochemical gunk, the sport is in danger of losing its traditional hands-on connection with nature. Too much of this stuff doesn't come from the woods anymore. You don't need to develop an eye for quality, and you certainly can't impress anyone by hauling out a rare patch of young, female, coastal Antron yarn.

Then again, maybe this is the wave of the future and therefore okay. If you release all the fish you catch, maybe it's entirely appropriate to fish with flies made of synthetics, even if they look a little phony. That way no living creature dies, and your credentials as a pacifist can remain impeccable. From that standpoint it's too bad that no one has even come close yet to making fake dry fly hackle.

For that matter, I sometimes think it sounds a little hollow to even talk about "natural" materials now that the word has become part of the meaningless gibberish of advertising. Now when you're told that something is 100 percent natural, the expectation is you'll buy it because you're stupid and easily buzzed.

Heating a house with a wood stove was natural (in the Madison Avenue sense) when I bought the place I live in. It was a statement in favor of self-reliance. Because it takes work, a chain saw, and a good truck to get the wood in yourself, it was a loud, public statement. You have to cut it, load it, haul it, unload it, split it, haul it again, stack it, and then carry it into the house five pieces at a time to burn. You have to learn how to vent the stove properly, clean out the ashes, and sweep the chimney. People can't help but see you doing all this.

It's an imposing list of chores. In fact, my sister was so impressed by her little brother's country ways that she sent me an American primitive-style ceramic plaque that read, HE WHO CUTS HIS OWN WOOD IS TWICE WARMED.

It's great to have a whole winter's worth of heat stacked neatly on the porch, out of the snow, where you can go and look at it. Great also to have a genuine heat source right there in the house, a real live fire in a cast-iron box surrounded by sleeping cats. It can be adjusted by stoking and venting the fire and/or moving your chair. It crackles, throws light, and demands attention. This is much more elemental than having wussy drafts of lukewarm air sneaking out of the walls, and then getting a bill once a month from a computer.

If you work at home, screwing around with the fire is a wonderful time killer.

If you're a fishing writer, you can talk honestly about tying flies with natural materials in front of the old wood stove, and generally come off as just organic as hell.

It all gets tied up together into what you now have to call a life-style.

But it's been taking some odd turns lately. First the Forest Service decided you needed a permit to cut wood on public land. Then cutting areas were restricted and the permit started to cost

money. Finally an FS guy admitted that they were now manag-
ing woodcutting (a job in the same class as shoveling manure) as
a "recreational experience."

Consequently, it got to be more trouble and expense than it
was worth, so I started buying my wood from a local woodcutter
who does it for a living.

Then there were the rumblings about forest management.
After all, there are only so many trees out there. What, exactly,
are they for? Last summer Ed, who was working for the Forest
Service, was fighting a fire near here. Someone said to him he
couldn't see working this hard to save the trees just so the FS
could turn around and sell them to a logging company.

"We're not," Ed said. "We're saving them so granola bars
like you can burn them up in their wood stoves and be
authentic."

Then there's the pollution. It came as a shock to some, but it
turns out that a significant amount of the air pollution in the
Denver area is caused by woodburning. Now several towns along
the front range ban the use of wood stoves and fireplaces on
officially proclaimed high pollution days, and legislators are
dancing around the idea of effectively banning wood heat
altogether in cities and towns by adding one regulation after
another until finally it's just too much of a pain in the ass.

I'm a long way from Denver, and there are no regulations
whatsoever out here in the county, but it's only a matter of time.
I'm already feeling the initial twinges of guilt.

In the winter, when the leaves are off the Russian olives, you
can see my woodpile from the road. It's beautiful. Pine, mostly,
but with some oak from Texas and some apple and cherry wood
I wangled from an orchard. Scrounging hardwood in a pine and
cottonwood state is something I'll miss.

It's fun to go out on a cold night in early February after a few
hours of flytying to get an armload of wood, and to see that
the pile is still plenty big enough to last till spring. But the time
will come when that beautiful woodpile is just a sign to the
smoke police that I'm one of those holdouts who should be
watched.

It's good to be a holdout, but only if you're in the right. You should also understand that holding out brings you a step closer to the day when you plop down in a rocking chair on the front porch with a shotgun in your lap and dare those whippersnappers to confront you with any more progress.

We'll probably all have to do that eventually, either individually or as a whole generation, but I, for one, would just as soon put it off for a while.

In other words, I'll eventually stop burning wood in the stove for the same reason I don't tie flies with condor feathers, and I won't complain too loudly either, because the logic in favor of both courses of action is inescapable. On the other hand, until deer, grouse, squirrels, and rabbits are endangered, I'll keep tying with natural materials.

It's a balancing act. You do what you can.

———

Speaking of which, my friend Mike Clark is doing what he can with jungle cock. This is the legendary bird that is probably the original ancestor of the modern domestic chicken, the one whose feathers in flytying mark the difference between "now" and "then" in the sport.

The cape feathers—called nails—from the gray jungle fowl were a traditional material for many streamers and salmon flies for generations. Because of that, the bird is now an endangered species. The feathers can't be imported and, although a licensed breeder can raise them domestically, he cannot kill his birds for any reason, least of all for flytying material.

I'm not kidding. Mike has just begun to raise these things, and he told me recently that when a bird dies the U.S. Department of Agriculture wants to see an autopsy report which had damned well better indicate natural causes.

So legal jungle cock nails for fly tying now have to be naturally molted feathers from live birds raised by licensed breeders. That means you have to go out every day in season and pick the feathers up off the ground lovingly, one by one, while praying that the wind doesn't blow.

They're worth about fifty cents apiece, and you need two per fly. Quantities are limited.

Mike is the kind of man who will do this, not so much for the money, but because he thinks it's neat, and because it helps to perpetuate the species. This is an esoteric sideline to his real business of building fine, handmade split bamboo fly rods.

There is still a small demand for jungle cock nails, mostly from tiers of salmon flies, although in general the flytying industry has left them behind. These feathers are very distinctive, and, although a number of things have been tried, most tiers feel there is no substitute. It's better just to leave them off than try to fake it. Better just to address the future.

I don't use them even though they can be gotten legally now because I don't care to add a dollar to the price of every streamer I tie, and because I don't care to be reminded that we fly-fishermen nearly extincted a species of bird because we thought their feathers were pretty. I'm embarrassed enough about that as it is.

On the other hand, it's been suggested that maybe we should use the stuff to encourage legal breeders to raise, and therefore save, the birds, paying the ungodly high price as a kind of restitution. After all, people like Mike aren't in the flytying material business, they're trying to do an ecological service, and maybe break even in the process.

I don't know if I'll end up using them or not. What I *do* know is that what was once an innocent, pretty little feather can now start a moral wrestling match. That, in turn, leads to the morning when you look out the window and think, Well, I still feel I'm right, but things have definitely changed—and not all for the better either.

You've known this was going to happen since you were fourteen years old, but it's still something of a blow when it happens.

—

I guess this came dangerously close to being the deadly story about "Things That Are Going Wrong with the Sport" but it was saved by the March '89 issue of *Fly Fisherman* magazine. There's a wonderful article in there by Art Lee about all the flies you can tie with wings made of the fur from the bottom of the hind foot of a snowshoe hare.

The snowshoe or varying hare is common, abundant, and widely hunted, but not all that easy to bag, being a white bunny sitting motionless in acres of snow.

I won't go into the whole rap, but apparently this is wonderful stuff, nothing else will do. Something about the natural oils makes it float beautifully, and something else about the material's consistency and the way sunlight plays in its texture makes trout mad for it. There is no substitute, natural or otherwise. For many patterns it's good right off the foot, for others it should be tinted with waterproof markers. But *don't dye it.* That would wash away, or at least dilute, the mysterious innate elixirs.

Of course, snowshoe hare feet aren't all that easy to come by, nor are they all the same. Mr. Lee says the best one he ever saw came from a hunter in Colorado, but he doesn't speculate as to what causes the difference in quality. Maybe it's the altitude, maybe it's the unfiltered solar radiation. It's a mystery.

This sounds just like the old days, and I love it.

I especially love it because I do a little snowshoe hare hunting in the winter myself, and so have access to the stuff. I haven't tied any flies with it yet, but I plan to. I've been saving the feet.

There are half a dozen dried hind feet on the desk in front of me right now. The hair is stiff, but not wiry. I'm told it holds its shape on a fly but is not especially difficult to work with.

On the bottom, most of the feet are a dirty, flat cream color, though some have a more yellowish cast, and two approach a subtle, pale dun. Given the coloring of most mayflies, these last two, presumably from the same animal, would be the most valuable.

What causes the difference in color? Age of the hare, maybe, or genetic heritage? More likely it's environmental. I know that essence of pine needle dissolved in a stagnant pond makes a kind of tea color, which might account for a yellowish cast on the feet of hares that run in pinewoods, while the feet of a hare that frequents rock piles might be stained dun by the lichens.

Who knows? It sounds right, and that's all it takes. I am in possession of a pair of extremely rare, natural pale dun Colorado rock-dwelling showshoe hare's feet. They're not for sale. These things are priceless.

CHAPTER 11

Guiding and Being Guided

 Let's get one thing straight right off the bat: I'm not a fishing guide. Never have been. Never will be. I don't enjoy it very much, and I'm not especially good at it. Most of the times I've tried guiding were when I weakened and gave in to flattery and/or the need for some fast money—two of the forces in nature that will make a person with a normally accurate self-image try to be something he's not, at least for a couple of days.

It hasn't been all bad, but I think I've done just enough of it now to get a feel for what it's like, and to know that I don't want to do it anymore.

The last time was one of the worst. A friend of mine who runs a combination guide service/fly-fishing school was short a hand one week, and in a serious bind with a big-tipping regular party due to show up in a couple of days. This was a somewhat trying bunch, he said, but still valuable, repeat customers. Would I please fill in? He'd pay me well, and consider it a personal favor if I'd help him out.

Okay, okay. If the truth were known, I sort of owed this guy a favor. It had also been awhile since I'd done any guiding. I knew I'd given it up, but didn't remember why quite vividly enough.

As I said, this was a guide service *and* school. I'm not much better at teaching fly-fishing than I am at guiding—I'm always saying encouraging, diplomatic things like, "No, you idiot, not like that, like this!"—but it was only for a few days. How bad could it be?

The sports in question were well-to-do professional people, most on the long end of middle age, who got together every summer for a few days of fly-fishing. I never determined exactly how many there were in the group because they were always getting split up this way and that among the staff, but I know there were no less than eight or nine of them. In other words, way too many for any kind of reasonable fishing trip.

They'd been doing this for a number of years, long enough for some personal traditions to develop, like the big fish fry on the last night.

A couple of days every season, and that's it. In one sense, they'd all been fly-fishing for years (that's what they'd tell you if you asked) but in another, much more meaningful sense, they had about a month's worth of experience between them. But then, they didn't *need* experience because they'd engaged a guide, you see.

The problem—both mine and theirs, but mostly mine—was that these people naturally wanted to catch some trout, but honestly didn't have any idea of how to go about it. Ten minutes after I'd met them, I, their steely-eyed, mountain man guide, had some doubts as to whether it was in the cards for them.

This is not a professional attitude. The Professional Attitude fairly reeks of confidence, enthusiasm, and rural good cheer.

I was sorry I'd taken it on, but there I was, so I waded in. I did, after all, know a little something about this.

For instance, you always start off calling your clients Mr. or Ms. So-and-So, although it's part of the implied social contract that they'll instruct you to drop that before the introductory handshake is released. A guide once told me, "If you say, 'Good morning, Mr. Smith,' and Mr. Smith doesn't say, 'Please, call me Bob,' it's gonna be a long day."

With this group it was "Mr." all around. That's how they

wanted it. It's what they were used to. Nobody wanted to be "Bob" to the help.

It's probably best not to ask what people do for a living. They may have traveled a long way to forget about all that, and, if not, they'll tell you all about it soon enough.

These guys never told me anything, probably because a fishing guide wouldn't have understood it, but I gathered from the conversation that it had something to do with small pieces of paper and large amounts of money.

You should also try to find out, politely, just how good your sports are at fly-fishing. You'll find that out soon enough, too, but it might help you decide where to take them.

The good ones will be modest—"Oh, I guess I do okay"—and a few duffers will lie to you as if you weren't going to see just how good or bad they are within the hour.

I also know that in the course of things it's acceptable to deliver short, bright, good-natured lectures on natural history, even with an environmental twist if you can keep from getting too strident, but you should refrain from arguing politics. If the client brings the subject up you can respond if, and *only* if, you agree. Even then, it's best to steer things in another direction. Most of us get mad when we think about politics, and angry people don't fish well. I know, I've tried it.

And you must always bear in mind what your assigned role is. You're an employee, though part of your job is to appear not to be an employee at all, but rather a sort of hybrid valet and fishing buddy. You are in charge and responsible if something goes wrong, otherwise the client is in charge.

You must also remember that you are not fishing, and I mean that literally and figuratively. If you carry a rod at all, it's used only for the occasional purpose of demonstration or, in a pinch, to search out fish or find the right fly. The client is fishing, *you* are guiding.

It's required that you at least smile at all jokes, even those involving members of ethnic groups in woodpiles.

And make no mistake about it: whatever the sport says, however realistic he seems, he expects you to make him catch fish. Lots of them. Big ones, too. He may or may not be willing to help you out with this.

As David Quammen said, the job demands "the humility of a chauffeur and the complacence of a pimp." If you decide to be a guide, I think you should do it for reasons other than that you love fishing.

———

With this particular bunch, I was guiding *and* teaching the basics of fly-fishing to a group who claimed to already know this stuff. Teaching is hard enough on the lawn with willing pupils. Trying to do it on a trout stream with fish rising and the pressure on is about as overwhelming as giving someone his or her first driving lesson in rush-hour traffic.

Furthermore, part of the job was to do this while staying out of the way and out of the conversation like a good waiter. This was, apparently, something of a reunion as well as a fishing trip, and everyone had a lot of catching up to do. For instance, since they'd seen each other last, most had gotten fax machines.

Then we'd arrive at the stream, the chatter would stop, and they'd all turn and look at me expectantly, as if to say, "All right, we're all ready to catch a fish now, if you please."

Yet another problem was that these people wanted to keep fish for the big fry on Saturday night, to which I was invited, of course. But the school was very catch-and-release oriented, which meant that this particular batch of people didn't fit into the usual program, and couldn't be taken to the usual spots. Naturally, the usual spots were the ones I knew the best. They were also where most of the trout lived.

It also meant that the single fish—large or small—couldn't be made into the genuine victory it should be for a beginner. There were mouths to feed, there was a working body count.

The first two days went well enough, considering the circumstances. That is, not many trout were caught, but no one drowned and I didn't get mad so you could tell. We broke the mob up among some of the other guides whenever possible, but

I never had fewer than four people, and the most any of them knew about fishing was that you had to hold the fat end of the rod.

A few things began to come back to me, like that old guys can't wade like younger guys, and that even younger guys can't wade very well when they only do it a few days every year. The bottom of a trout stream isn't much like a sidewalk. Even on a relatively small stream I had to physically place these people in their casting positions, and then come back to lead them out when they wanted to move, which was often. If one of them didn't hook a fish in five minutes it was because I hadn't put him in the right spot.

I also remembered that you shouldn't spread inexperienced sports out too much along the stream because, what with the more or less constant attention they all require, you'll end up jogging twenty miles by lunchtime—over boulders, in waders.

Basically, these men were the worst kind of clients you could have: the kind real guides must have nightmares about. Simply put, they couldn't fish, didn't care to learn, but still expected to catch trout without trying.

They wouldn't even make a stab at casting to the spots I pointed out, nor would they pay attention to any of my attempts at casting instructions because, as any of them would point out, while peeling tangled fly line from their hats, they already knew how to cast. In fact, they ignored just about all my suggestions, which got gradually more forceful as time went on.

One guy insisted on fishing a size 8 Rat-faced McDougal through a hatch of #16 cream-colored caddis flies because he had once caught a fish on this very fly. And the fly looked it.

Naturally, I had to tie it to his leader for him.

At every break they'd all gather around the brand-new Styrofoam cooler that was supposed to be filling up with trout for the much discussed gala fish fry, which, I began to realize, was the real reason for the trip. By lunchtime on the second day we had five or six pitiful little rainbows and one ten-inch brown. They wanted many more fish; I wasn't too pleased with those we had already.

When the man who seemed to be the spiritual leader of the group asked me where all the trout were, not to mention the big ones, I admitted that they were mostly in the catch-and-release area where we couldn't go because we were killing fish.

That was a mistake. If I hadn't said anything they never would have known.

"I'll tell you what," he said, "why don't you take us there, just so we can land a few nice ones before it's all over."

"Well," I said, "I didn't say you could catch them, just that they were in there."

This amounted to insubordination, and I could tell the guy didn't appreciate it, but I couldn't help myself. A real guide would have thought that, but he wouldn't have said it.

So, against my advice and better judgment, we ended up in the catch-and-release area where my troop continued to cast like bored children—fishing the wrong places with the wrong flies—and failed to catch trout that were noticeably larger than the ones they had failed to catch earlier. Now and then one of them would glance at me as if to say, "Well . . . aren't you going to *do* something?" and I'd look back as if to say, "What more *can* I do?"

Mostly I was hoping no one I knew would see me.

But even no-kill water breeds its share of stupid fish, and the leader managed to hook a nice one on his enormous Rat-faced McDougal, which pleased him immensely because it seemed to be proof that I'd been wrong about that. I ran downstream to help him land it, but he wanted to do it himself. I have to admit, he managed it rather smoothly, using my net.

It was a lovely, deep-bodied female rainbow of about sixteen inches with a forest green back, ink-black pepper spots all over, and the bright red stripe down its side that marks a wild fish. She was lovely, a real knockout.

"I'm going to keep this one," he announced, reaching for his aluminum stringer.

"Ah, look," I said, "as I mentioned before, this is a catch-and-release area, so you *can't* keep the fish. It would be illegal."

He looked down at the trout. He was holding it way too

tightly. This was a man who had grown used to getting what he wanted, a man for whom the rules ought to move aside of their own accord.

"Come on," he said, "what would really happen if I kept it?"

I considered that. It was pretty obvious.

"What would happen is, your guide would drive into town, turn you in to the ranger, and you'd get your sorry ass busted."

That was either the wrong thing to say, or exactly the right thing. I still don't honestly know, but I *do* know why I don't guide anymore.

———

When I said I knew something about this, I meant the easy stuff, the etiquette and the posture. That is, under pressure I was able to look and act like a guide. On the water, where it counts, I always prayed for a moderately competent fisherman, half a break from the trout, and then just tried to be a decent caddie, but there is much more to it than that.

For instance, a good guide not only knows how to fish, he is also able to translate that information quickly into terms that are available to all manner of people. Those are two very distinct skills, especially considering the variety of clients you deal with.

You'll get fishermen who don't have a clue; others who *do* have a clue, but little else; all the way up to guys who are so good you wonder why they wasted money on a guide in the first place.

The very best client to have is a jolly, flamboyant tipper who's just happy to be out of the office and who doesn't much care if he catches a trout or not. The second best, and the most fun, is the one who actually knows how to fish. Chances are you won't see many of either in a season.

The thing I always had the most trouble figuring out was the appropriate level at which to intrude. Some people want to be led by the hand through the entire operation, and be complimented profusely even on their mistakes, as in, "Hey, I've seen people hook their ears a lot more often than you do." That's dreary work, but at least you know what's expected of you. On the other end of the scale is the guy who is alone with his muse even in a crowd.

This guy wants to locate his own fish, select his own flies, tie his own knots, and land and release his own trout. He's into solitude, so he isn't up for much conversation, he's noticed the scenery, thank you, and he already knows the names of all the birds. He must want you there because he hired you, but it never becomes clear what the hell you're supposed to do. Just stand there and hold the sandwiches, I guess. After a while you're tempted to go back to the truck and take a nap, but, if nothing else, you understand that you're not being paid to sleep.

You have your professional pride. The only thing worse than having a client get skunked is drowning him or getting him eaten by a bear, but if you flutter around and talk too much, you're intrusive: a pain in the neck. If you hang back too much, you're lazy and/or incompetent. To be good you have to do it just right. With any luck, the sport will at least give you a hint.

———

In recent seasons—luckily, for everyone concerned—I've spent more time as the client, and the one thing that doing a little bit of guiding in the past has taught me is how to be guided.

A lot of it has to do with getting things straight, most of which can be done in advance. Do you want to be pampered or worked? Be honest. Do you want to catch lots of fish, or do you want to go for the few hogs? You probably won't get it both ways. Be up front about it, and then let your guide locate the balance point between what you want and what you can fairly expect.

If you just want to see the river and catch some fish, fine. If you do have something special in mind, tell the guide, especially if you feel strongly about it. He may be good, but he's not psychic.

"If I can't catch 'em on dry flies I don't want to fish," you say.

"You gotta use nymphs here," the guide replies.

Maybe that's true and maybe it's not, and maybe you're some

kind of stuck-up purist who'll never be happy. Whatever, this is not your guide. Maybe it's not even your river.

There will be times when you have to consciously put yourself in a guide's hands: to accept his guidance. The better you are at fly-fishing (or the better you think you are) the harder this is, so the trick is to overcome your ego. Okay, you know rivers, but this is a new one with its own little idiosyncrasies, and maybe you don't actually know everything.

It was like that when A.K. and I fished with Russ Kipp on the Beaverhead in Montana a few years ago. In the stretch we floated, the river is deep, fast, and narrow, with tight, overhanging willows along most of the banks. It's not exactly like a tunnel because you can see the sky. It's more like a deep, green ditch with a river in the bottom of it. The evening before we went out Russ told us what it would be like:

The rubber raft will be moving quickly in the main current. The trout will be tight to the banks, under the willows. You get one cast per spot at close range, so it's going to be fast and furious. Russ told us to dig out our heaviest rods and overline them by one size so they'd load up with very little line in the air. There would be none of this namby-pamby false casting. Leaders should be short, level, and heavy, both to handle big browns in fast current and to get streamers back from the willows.

It doesn't matter how accurate a caster you are, you will hang up in the brush, and there will be no going back for flies or slowing down while you tie on a new one.

"This is what we call 'Montana-crude' fly-fishing," Russ said.

The locally accepted streamer pattern was a huge, heavy thing with lots of rubber hackle called a French Tickler. A properly tied French Tickler casts like a banana, sinks like a stone, and is deadly to fish who bite it and to fishermen who get hit with one.

So early the next morning we began shooting down the river, with Russ at the oars slowing the drift as much as he could, and calling out the spots along each bank as they came up. "Nice eddy on the left, under the branch, ahead of the rock . . ." You'd get one cast, which had to be accurate, a second for the fly to sink, another second or two for a twitch, and then you were into either a fish or the next cast.

When a fly hooked brush, Russ would yell "Down!" and everyone would duck as the stuck fisherman pointed his rod straight at the snag and the weight of the raft broke it loose. It was pretty menacing, even if all that came back was the leader.

Russ said it was a little slow, but we caught enough fish, and each one gave us a nip-and-tuck fight right to the net, if we could get him that far.

I remember focused concentration and a sore casting arm. What I don't remember, unfortunately, is much about how the river looked while we were on it. All I really saw of it was a rolling close-up showing a band of water and a band of brush, now and then punctuated by the yellow flash of a brown trout.

Scenery aside, it was great, one of the wildest days of fishing we've ever had. We still talk about it when the fishing gets intense, "Remember the Beaverhead?" The point is, without a guide who knew how it worked, we'd have peered down that tunnel of brush and fast water, shrugged, and driven on to the next river. If nothing else, we needed his boat just to get in there.

———

Now and then you'll hire a guide and that's about all you'll get: a boat and someone to row it.

Three years ago a few of us took a two-day float down a big Colorado trout river that had what Ed Engle calls a high remoteness factor. In this one stretch it flows through a deep, sheer-sided gorge, complete with some horrifying rapids. In a section that takes two days to float, there are only a handful of places where a fisherman on foot—or maybe on horseback—can get down into it to fish some pitifully small pieces of water that are isolated by vertical rock walls and deep water on both ends.

It's a good trout river, fished almost exclusively from big, inflatable rafts.

The man we floated it with was a fine river runner, a big,

strapping oarsman who digs rapids and who is, without doubt, the captain of the ship. You wear your flotation vest, and it's buckled all the way to the top, never mind how hot it is. When he says, "Sit down and grab hold of something," you do it without asking why. It will become obvious in a matter of seconds.

But all he knew about fishing was that the trout are in the river somewhere, and people with rods and funny hats sometimes catch them. When he advertised guided fishing trips, he meant that he'd run you down the river, and if you wanted to fish on the way, then that was okay with him.

I had my first suspicions at the put-in point while we were waiting for some other parties to get going.

"So," I said, "what are you getting them on?"

"Well," he answered, "flies, I guess, or some guys use spinners."

"I see. It's browns and rainbows, isn't it?"

"I think so," he said, and then called down to another guide who was getting his party situated. "Browns and rainbows in here, right?"

It wasn't bad. In fact, it was fun to take charge of the boat for a change, and to air out every fisherman's fantasy, the one where you know more than the guide. At first we made suggestions: "Think you could get a little closer to the bank through here?" but gradually we became more assured and the suggestions became orders: "Okay, get us into that backwater over there."

Fly patterns and tactics we had to figure out for ourselves, but that was fun, too. The more you do for yourself, the more credit you can take if you connect with some trout.

When we'd come around a bend in the gorge and an ominous rumbling would begin to build in the air, command of the ship would instantly revert to the guide.

"Reel in and grab something," he'd say, "This one is called 'The Grim Reaper,' class five rapids." This was his thing, and he loved it.

At a time like that it's perfectly acceptable that the man on the oars knows more about white water than he does about fishing.

—

I think what a good guide does is to somehow gain purchase on the situation almost immediately, and then, with a touch so light it's imperceptible, he steers things right. When it works it's a wonderful thing to behold. In the end, the client feels as if he did it all himself because, except for a gentle nudge here and there, he did. I can't be any more specific than that. If I could, I'd be able to do it myself. The best I can do is appreciate it.

There are fishermen who don't care to use guides. Some say that being guided cheats them out of that sense of exploration and discovery. Others just don't like to shell out the money, although they'll mine all the free information they can at the local fly shop.

A lawyer friend of mine is adamant. "I won't pay for guides or hookers," he says. "There are some things a man should arrange for himself."

—

A friend of mine who does walk-and-wade guiding trips on a very good trout river once told me a story about "the old man." He showed up at the fly shop one day in a long, black limo, driven by a tall, dark chauffeur who opened the door, tipped his cap, nodded when spoken to, never let anything like an expression brighten his face, and never spoke. Not exactly sinister, but a little spooky.

Everyone in the shop went to the windows to gawk. "Who is this?" someone asked.

The old man himself was seriously old, approaching ancient, easily into his seventies or better, but who can really tell? You certainly don't ask. My friend described him as small, frail, shaky, walking slowly and breathing shallowly.

What the guy wanted was to catch a twenty-inch rainbow on a dry fly, and to that specific end he had arrived on a fine stream during the Green Drake hatch. In the right place and at the right time, in other words, which at least gives you a leg up on the dreaded Client with the Special Goal in Mind.

My friend, always the professional, said, "Yes sir, I'll do my best," while thinking, Christ, I hope he lives through the day.

It doesn't happen often, but clients do just drop dead now and then.

The old man got into his waders by himself, slowly. They were good canvas waders, worn, but with no patches. A guy who arrives on the river in a limousine would not have his waders patched. At the first sign of a leak he'd have the butler phone Orvis to order a new pair. Custom fitted, of course. They'd have his measurements on file.

The rod was a light bamboo, handmade by a famous rod maker who is no longer with us. It was in a leather-covered rod tube with a brass nameplate on it. My friend didn't recognize the name, but thought maybe he should. When someone shows up in a big, black Lincoln with tinted windows, you can't help wondering, along with the crowd back in the shop, "Who the hell *is* this, anyway?" A financier? Spy? Gangster?

The man spoke very little. He wasn't sullen, he wasn't stuck up, and he wasn't dingy. He just didn't seem to have a whole lot to say.

My friend took the man to the quietest water he could think of where the big mayflies would still be hatching, and tied the locally approved Green Drake dry fly to the man's leader because he made no move to do it himself. The man nodded his thanks, and then tested the knot.

The hatch came off well that day, and trout rose eagerly, although, as usual, they were careful and picky, needing a good drift before they'd strike.

The old guy, my friend said, was a wonderful caster of that gracious, Old World, wood rod style where the elbow is kept at the side, as if you were holding a Bible under your arm. It was slow, graceful, effortless, and accurate: the kind of casting you don't see anymore.

And yes, the old man caught fish. As it turned out, he was very good at this.

By the time the hatch was about to peter off, the man had landed a number of nice trout—had, in fact, put in a very respectable day—but the twenty-incher on the dry fly had eluded him. Nothing was said, but my friend hadn't forgotten about that, and something in the old man's bearing indicated that he hadn't forgotten either.

Up to now, the guide had done little more than watch and occasionally change a fly, but now he spoke up.

"Right over there," he said, pointing, "far bank, in the little curl of current just up from the bridge, see the big head coming up?"

The old man looked at the spot until the trout rose again, nodded, and began wading toward the main current. The cast would have to be across and downstream into slack water. To get the right drift, the caster would have to be standing in some pretty fast, deep current. My friend didn't feel that he should take the man by the arm, so he waded in next to him on the downstream side so he could at least grab him if he went in. This guy was as dry and brittle as old newspaper; in fast current he could dissolve.

The man wobbled precariously a few times, but he stayed upright and got to where he had to be.

The first cast was brilliant, the drift flawless, and the fish took so slowly and casually it would have broken your heart if you'd seen it. The old man set the hook just right—not too soon, not too late, not too hard.

This was the twenty-inch rainbow on a dry fly. In fact, it was more like a twenty-four-incher.

The fight was long, and not what you'd call one-sided, but it came to a point where the big, strong trout was below the bridge and the frail old fisherman was above, with some deep, treacherous wading in between where the current sluiced between the pilings.

The old man started under the bridge, shuffling, leaning into the current, and the guide said, "Uh, listen, would you like me to run down there and net him for you?"

"What I'd like," the old man said, "is for you to keep your goddamned hands off my fish."

"Yes sir," my friend said.

Whoever this guy was, he was definitely someone you'd call "sir."

CHAPTER 12

THE CHAIRMAN'S BASS

This happened roughly twenty years ago, give or take a season. I suppose I could figure it out exactly, but it doesn't really matter. Let's just say it was in the old days.

I was in my early twenties, living on the outskirts of Boulder, Colorado, in a place that had once been a tourist motel, but was by then rented dirt cheap by the month. It was a pretty place, in an Appalachian sort of way: apparently handmade from smooth river rocks and cement, not up to building code in any number of ways, and having seen plenty of better days. Even when new it would have been considered, at best, rustic.

In the custom of the times, those of us who lived in the seven old units fell into a kind of loose communal situation. We shared a vegetable garden out back, fed each other's dogs, took messages for each other on the pay phone out in the dirt courtyard, and operated a primitive form of the car pool whereby the person whose vehicle happened to be running that week was the chauffeur.

There was an open field to the south, a ranch pasture to the east, another field to the west, and a modest creek lined with stately old cottonwoods flowing by to the north. It may have been just barely in, or just barely past, the city limits.

The creek was just a little too far from the foothills to be very good, but there were sometimes trout in it in the spring and early summer that had washed down from upstream plantings, and we were not above harvesting and eating some of them. The same went for the fox squirrels up in the trees and the cottontail rabbits on the ground. In season, of course.

These were the beginnings of a kind of subsistence period, during which I ("we," that is, it was always "we") lived what seemed like a simple, marginally self-sufficient life while waiting for the sick, evil society out there to spontaneously restructure itself in our image.

Maybe you remember that late sixties version of the hopeful innocence of youth where the future was so shaky it was exciting. We were more than a little naive, but life wasn't bad.

The place is gone now, as are just about all the cheap places to live in Boulder. It was condemned and torn down, and then the town crept out and sucked up the vacant lot that was left behind by the bulldozers. Where my old black-and-tan coon hound was buried, there is now either a four-lane highway or the parking lot for an office building. I can't locate the exact spot any more than I can tell you exactly what year it was. As I said, it was the old days.

I had a respectable job then mowing the rough at a golf course. At five-thirty on Monday morning I'd start at point A, pulling a gang of mowers behind an old but serviceable John Deere tractor. I'd mow through Saturday, have Sunday off, and, if it all went according to schedule, I'd start back at point A on Monday and do it all over again. Endlessly, at the minimum wage.

It was okay. At the time I was either a Zen Buddhist or an existentialist, I forget which, and I was off early enough in the day to fish the afternoons and evenings.

There were the usual ponds scattered around the course, and, having a thing for water, I'd always manage to take my scheduled and unscheduled breaks next to them. I'd noticed some little bluegills in these things from time to time, and even a couple of small bass, but had never given the ponds much serious thought because I didn't like where they were.

I've never cared for the game of golf, or mowed grass for that matter, especially when I had to mow it. I thought then (and still do) that fishing should be done in places that are, if not actually wild, then at least unmanicured. I could fish other warm-water ponds that were nearby, and a lot more pleasant, too, so the fish at the golf course were nothing more than a mildly interesting curiosity.

Then, one early morning when I was having a bit of trouble getting wired up for a whole day of mowing, I stopped not ten minutes into the shift to watch a particularly handsome blue heron wading the pond out by the back fence, and saw the boil of an enormous largemouth bass. And I mean enormous.

You know how that is. Even in water you take seriously, you somehow don't want to believe it. Half of your mind says That had to be a big bass, and the other half replies, No, it had to be a carp, or maybe a muskrat. It was just too *big*. These were just water traps, after all.

The evidence itself is gone in a matter of a few seconds, so you're left trying to make the final determination based on the notoriously faulty short-term memory of a fisherman.

It made the diagnostic chugging sound of a bass, right? And what you saw of the back was bass green instead of carp yellow, right?

You understand I had to know for sure, so I pulled my rig over to where the angle of the light and the view seemed about right, and feigned a mechanical problem with one of the mowers.

The foreman was a Republican with eyes like a hawk, and he was of the opinion that everyone in the world except him was lazy and good for nothing, especially guys whose hair was a little on the long side. Still, the machinery was old, and as long as you had a wrench in your hand there wasn't much he could say. I would always have just gotten the thing tightened back up about the time he was a hundred yards away.

By the time I had the whole gang of mowers adjusted properly—and the foreman's pickup was just leaving the shop in my direction—I had managed to see the fish a few times; never very well, but enough to know that it was, in fact, a largemouth bass, easily eight pounds, maybe pushing ten.

Okay, fine. Now back to work. The foreman stopped his pickup as I climbed onto the tractor seat. He sat there glaring at me, gunning the engine.

Now the sighting of a big fish is the sort of thing that can gnaw on you, especially when you're doing a repetitive job outside in hot weather with no one to talk to for hours at a time. However long you fish, you never get over the astonishment of spotting the game, and thinking, Oh, shit, *there he is*!

I couldn't help mulling it over, and later that day I almost piled into a tree while mowing around the next pond because I was watching the water instead of where I was going. There wasn't so much as a single sign of life in that one, but then it was the middle of a summer day when small ponds snooze.

I figured I hadn't seen that bass before because he was largely nocturnal, and I had never been at that particular pond quite that early in the morning before. What I'd seen were probably the last, half-interested pickings of a whole night of feeding. The fish *had* seemed sort of apathetic, as if he was already full, but still going through the motions.

I can't say the golf course started to look like a prettier place to fish, but I ended up wanting that bass.

When I punched out at the end of the day I asked the foreman, as casually as possible, if anyone ever fished the ponds. Just curious, you know?

"You seen one of the chairman's bass, didn't ya?" he said.

I felt as if I'd been caught poaching already, but I asked him to explain that, which he did briefly and pointedly.

"The chairman of the board put them fish in there, and him and his friends are the only ones who can fish here, understand?"

"You bet," I said, realizing that I'd made the mistake of tipping my hand.

The foreman and I never did get to be what you'd call pals.

Maybe that's why I never got around to catching that bass: because the jig was already up. I can remember some of the things I did, or decided not to do, twenty years ago, but not always what my reasoning was like.

I do remember planning it, though.

I'd go over the back fence at two in the morning—or maybe three—at a spot that was only thirty yards or so from the pond across open ground. I'd have to stay low, but once at the water my silhouette would be camouflaged by trees.

My truck would be parked a half mile away with the hood up so any passing police would take it for an abandoned vehicle. That would be believable. The thing looked like an abandoned vehicle even when I was driving it.

I only owned a few fly rods then, but there was an old taped-together fiberglass eight-footer fitted with a worn-out reel that could be expendable if worse came to worst and I had to chuck it in the bushes.

I'd have one size 2 deer hair mouse tied to a level thirty-pound test leader. No fly changes, no long, sporting fight. This was going to be a quick, well-planned assassination.

It never occurred to me that I wouldn't be able to get this bass. The fish was fat, pampered, indifferent, and, most importantly, undisturbed. The chairman might cast a spoon in there two or three times a year, but he would be an aging dilettante who would not fish long, hard, well, or even at the right time of day. I knew that with the certainty of youth.

That fish was stupid, and he was mine for the taking.

I hadn't planned a crime since I was ten years old and a couple of us laid out what we thought would be a neat bank job. There was one difference: at ten you know you won't really do it, at twenty-something, you're not so sure.

But I didn't do it, as I mentioned, and as you probably guessed from the fact that I'm even relating all this. I wish I could say I arrived at my current opinion on such things then, but those developments are usually more gradual. At that time I think I assumed that any American capitalist with the title "chairman" preceding his name was a fascist lackey who didn't deserve a ten-pound bass. Game fish to the people. Now I think anyone with the foresight to surreptitiously put some bass in ponds that he alone is likely to fish is probably a guy I could get along with, and who is, therefore, someone who might invite me to come right in through the front gate to fish if he was cajoled in the proper way.

And if that sounds too noble, then, yes, I was afraid of getting caught, too. Okay?

———

Private water. It's always bluer and deeper, with bigger, dumber fish. That's one of the myths you live by as a fisherman, and it's a fair enough bet.

It's also a fair bet that the higher the fence and the more menacing the signs, the better the fishing would be if you could get on. A terse KEEP OUT on three strands of barbed wire is one thing, while TRESPASSERS WILL BE PROSECUTED TO THE FULLEST EXTENT OF THE LAW on chain link is quite another, "fullest" (rather than just "full") being the kind of overstatement a lawyer would use.

You see, there's some subliminal manipulation going on here.

There are lots of different styles. Some landowners prefer the warning followed with "by order of the sheriff of such-and-such county." That has an officious look and ring to it, while a hand-painted NO FISHING, DON'T EVEN ASK is more down-home serious and probably more immediately dangerous.

I'll point out that only that last one actually prohibits asking permission, although some of the others hint pretty strongly at the answer you'll get.

In some places you need a translator. Up in Montana they often post property by painting orange stripes on the fence poles. My friend Dave Carty says that if the paint is faded, it means "I'm not as upset about this as I was a couple of years ago. Maybe we can discuss it," while a fresh coat of fluorescent paint indicates that there is a .270 trained on your temple at this very moment. Don't make no sudden movements, and do not come up to the house.

There are different styles of what we'll call management, too.

Sometimes access, even to very good water, is surprisingly negotiable. "Hi," you say—if you can locate the owner—"can we fish here?" and the possibility exists that he'll say, "Yeah, okay, just close the gates behind you."

"Really?" you say. "Jeeze, thanks."

That sort of thing still happens. I make it work—or maybe I should say it *just works* through the grace of the gods—a couple of times every season. Of course, it's part of the implied contract that I don't tell you where.

Let's just say there's a gorgeous bass and panfish pond hereabouts that I can get on if I go with the guy who actually has permission to fish there. This is absolutely mythical private water in which both species of fish are twice the size of the ones you'll catch in the nearby public ponds, and so easy to fool you really can get weary of it after a while. By prior agreement, we keep nothing. Whatever thinning the populations need is done by the owner.

Going in secondhand, on someone else's coattails, involves the kind of clumsy scheduling arrangements that prevent you from spontaneously deciding that today would be a good day to fool around with some three-quarter-pound panfish, or maybe that you'd like to fish there by yourself for a change. With that in mind, I've toyed with the idea of asking for permission myself. I'll have to sit down and quietly work that one out sometime. Without being able to quite put my finger on the principle, it sounds vaguely unethical.

It was on the coattails of Jackson Streit, a fishing guide in Breckenridge, Colorado, that I got onto a fine stretch of river that's owned by a seriously private fishing club. The showpiece here is brown trout of tremendous size that move up from a reservoir downstream in the fall to spawn. As I recall, the club rules said you couldn't keep one under twenty-five inches, or something like that. You get the idea.

It can get spotty—these are brown trout, after all—and the very best of it is seasonal, but it can be so good you get casual about it.

The day we fished it I watched Jackson hook a huge brown

that had chased his streamer to within inches of the bank we were standing on before striking. When he felt the hook, the fish jumped once and landed with a dull plop on the sand at our feet. There he lay, dead still, gazing into the cloudy sky, lost and amazed in the wrong element. Jackson calmly reached down, unhooked the fish, and nudged him back into the stream.

The trout was, I'd guess, twenty-two inches long, not even a keeper, and the whole drama had taken five seconds. No photos, no backslapping.

"The trick," Jackson said, "is to land them quickly."

———

A few years ago in Montana, A.K. and I fell in with a guy named Bill Crabtree. Crabtree spends his summers in and around West Yellowstone and is what you'd have to call a seasonal local. He's one of those rare guys who fishes long, hard, and very well, but who never seems to get either grim or fanatical about it.

In a few short days of fishing with him we'd learned the simple truth that if we went where he went and did what he did, we'd catch fish, so when he asked us one morning if we'd like to go see about some rainbow/cutthroat hybrids in a little lake he knew about, A.K. said, "Lead on."

The lake was owned by a mummified widower cowboy who was at least a hundred years old, who lived in a house of roughly the same vintage that you'd swear was abandoned, even when you were standing on the front porch. Absolutely authentic, and in the middle of nowhere, too. The lake was not visible from the road.

There were the usual curt introductions, followed by the regulation half hour of shit-kicking, scratching, and inquiring after the health of the cattle and the relatives. Bill said that, naturally, we wouldn't be keeping any fish, to which the cowboy replied "Yup" as if he'd heard this before, and believed it, but still didn't understand it.

A.K. and I stood around trying not to seem too impatient, and when the money for the privilege of fishing there finally changed hands, it was so quick and subtle it could have been a street corner drug deal.

As we were turning to go the cowboy said, "By the way, if you catch that big one, kill him for me, will you? He's been eating up too many of the smaller trout and I'd like him outta there."

"Uh, how big is the 'big one'?" I asked. (The obvious question.)

"Last time I seen him, maybe thirty inches. You'll recognize him."

———

Not all private water is fabulous, but, as I said, it can be a fair bet—something worth looking into.

There are those who enjoy the commercial fish-for-pay places, like Armstrong's and Nelson's spring creeks in Montana, for their ambience of exclusivity and privilege. I don't have a lot of experience with joints like that, but they're really not bad as a change of pace, as long as you understand that you're buying "good fishing" rather than actually purchasing trout. You know the fish are there (you've been hearing about them for years), you know it won't be crowded, and you know you can get on because you have, of all things, a reservation. Because of the relatively stable nature of spring creeks, the fishing will be as predictable as it's likely to get, and the money (I think the average is about thirty dollars per rod, per day) isn't bad.

Incidentally, it's referred to as "renting a rod on the creek" but the fee is for simple access. There's a story about a dude who showed up, paid his money, and then asked, "Okay, where's my fishing pole?"

"You're supposed to bring your own," he was told.

Back when I was contemplating poaching the chairman's bass I had never paid to fish and figured I never would. Fishing that wasn't free may or may not have been a fascist plot to enslave the masses, but it violated my personal aesthetic and so I had a rule against it.

I guess I was still working out the morality of coveting my neighbor's bass.

The personal rules aren't as strict now, and I'll pay for it when I have the money to spare and when I think it's worth it. I've never done the two big spring creeks—Nelson's and Armstrong's—because they're booked too far in advance, and I just never seem to know what I'll be up to that far in the future.

I've done DePey's (pronounced "DeePews") spring creek and it was great: a small, weed-choked stream full of trout, funky fisherman's shack with a picture window, wood stove and fly-tying desk, and a genuine river keeper named Robert Auger who seemed to enjoy his work immensely. It's a lesser-known creek in the same beautiful Yellowstone Valley with Nelson's and Armstrong's. There are Russell Chatham landscapes everywhere you look, and you can get on the water sooner than two years from now.

It was completely satisfactory, but I know I'll never make a habit of it. I'm not exactly sure why.

Deciding how you feel about this inevitably leads you to wonder, Why do I do this in the first place? and I'm not sure about that either, although it's a fair, if self-indulgent, question.

I guess I don't know why I fish in any really definitive sense. I've written a couple of books about the whys of it, and it occurs to me now that I fish, in part, so I can write books like that. If nothing else, it beats mowing the rough at the golf course.

And then there's the mythology of it, which is considerable. The fisherman is "out there" looking around, figuring it out, restless, and mobile, and he knows about these places, you see. Places you and I *don't* know about, and couldn't get on if we did. The fisherman is plugged in somehow.

Like Dave Carty in Bozeman, Montana. Dave has only lived there for a few years, but he's already developed an enviable network of places to fish and hunt. He's a relentless scouter and talker who can get on all kinds of private land without paying for it, unless you count the odd bottle of whiskey and the Christmas cards.

Unlike Bill Crabtree, Carty *is* a little feverish about it, but he's also young, and he has such a shameless good time at it that it's not only okay, it's infectious. Driving off in his camper before dawn some morning—seventy miles an hour on a back road, honking at the deer—the conversation will go dead for a few minutes, and Dave can be heard muttering, "Fish an' hunt, hunt an' fish . . ."

And then he's back: "We'll hit that stretch on So-and-So's place, and if it's not happening there we can drive up to the such-and-such ranch, or maybe old what's-his-name will let us on if he's home. Hey, did I remember to buy gas last night?"

Maybe what I'm saying is, private water can be wonderful, poaching is unacceptable, and paying for it is too easy. These things need to be done correctly.

———

One of my clearest memories from childhood is of prowling around midwestern backroads with my uncle Leonard asking people if we could fish, and getting answers in the affirmative as often as not, plus maybe something like, "And bring me a couple of fish if you get any."

In each particular case it was because we either knew the guy already, or we asked politely and looked harmless enough, or the man was having a decent day and felt generous, or, perhaps, that he could stand some fish for the table, but didn't have the time to go get them himself.

In a general sense, it *was* because he didn't have the time himself. These guys were farmers, not sport fishermen, and, although farming when I was a kid wasn't the desperate enterprise it is now, it was still a damned hard job that required long hours and a sharp eye for not wasting anything. There was fishing because there had to be water for the stock, and once there was a pond full of water, well, you might as well make use of it and toss some fish in. If you didn't already know how it worked, the county extension agent would line it up for you: a few basic, easy-to-meet physical requirements, plus X pounds of bluegills and X pounds of bass per surface acre and you were in business.

Now they'd call it an ancillary use of an existing resource, which is just newspeak for common sense.

It was all private, but it seems to have been arranged so that there were obvious, even intentional, chinks in the armor. This was in the old days, too, when it was not yet generally accepted that any courteous stranger could be a serial killer.

Part of the implied social contract went like this: if the guy says no, you say "thanks, anyway" and move on. He doesn't owe you an explanation. It's his pond, and they're his fish, just like that big, beautiful bass, like it or not, belonged to the chairman.

CHAPTER 13

RIVERS

Henry's Fork of the Snake: It's the second week in August, the middle of the so-called off season here, and there's almost no one around, even though the Callibaetis mayflies are falling on the water down by Osborn Bridge every morning around nine o'clock. This event, someone decided without consulting you, is not considered to be one of the better hatches on this river, and so, for the moment at least, the mob has departed.

More than anything, it's strange. The K.O.A. Campground in Last Chance is all but deserted; the famous Green Drake water upstream from the Railroad Ranch is empty except for that one gull that's always perched on Bird Rock; guides are working other rivers; fly shop owners are drinking coffee and waiting patiently for the September crowds.

This is a big river, but not an intimidating one. In the flats above the bridge it's wide, slow, sleepy-looking, and eminently wadable in most spots, with waist-deep water and a hard sand bottom. You get dunked only when you get too casual, or too engrossed, and simply walk into a channel. This happens more often than you'd think.

Right through here the river splits into three channels. The land is flat, but mountains are visible in every direction that affords a view. To the east you can see all the way to the Red Mountains in Yellowstone Park across an open sagebrush meadow where sandhill cranes strut. To the west the pine forest comes right down to the water and leans in on the bends.

This is navigable water, the bottom end of a good float through the Railroad Ranch stretch, but on this trip you haven't seen a boat in days, and only a few other wading fishermen who looked dwarfed by the scenery.

It's more than strange, it's eerie. A famous river, a clockwork spinner fall, big trout rising under overcast skies that make them confident and casual, and only three other fishermen in the last five days. Granted, the afternoons and evenings have been a little slow—caddis hatches have been off and the hoppers aren't really doing it—but what do you want, nonstop action? "No," your partner admits as you sit in camp one day, tying up more Speckled Spinners to replace the ones you've left in fish, "I guess that's not what I really want after all."

The guy at the fly shop, who has plenty of time to talk right now, says, "Sure, there are more rising fish at other times of year, but there are more rising fish *per fisherman* now. You guys are probably doing this exactly right."

Dropping the "probably," you let that ring in your head: "You guys are doing this exactly right."

———

Frying Pan: Basalt, Colorado, qualifies as a bona fide trout town because, for a population of less than a thousand people, it has two fly shops and a sporting goods store, and because when you walk down Main Street in neoprene waders no one asks you if those are some kind of ski pants. That kind of thing will sometimes happen up the road in Aspen.

You don't spend much time in town because you're always busy fishing the Frying Pan River, but after many seasons you've come to know the place a little, largely through trips in from the campground for supplies, and the occasional café breakfast or celebratory dinner and drinks.

The Pan is a quick, jumbled river in a steep, bright, rufous-colored canyon with lots of trees. On a clear day it's red, green, and ice-water blue. In the fourteen miles from Ruedi Dam to the confluence with the Roaring Fork, you'll find every kind of water you'd ever want to fish. The trout are very big.

In February you check into a motel, using as an excuse the fact that the Little Maud Campground up by the dam is closed for the winter, but secretly relieved to have a warm, dry place to sleep after those cold days on the river. The woman behind the desk tells you, without being asked, that the river is fishing well and they're getting them on midges. This kind of information gets around on a daily basis; it's part of the mass consciousness of the town.

The desk clerk may or may not be a fisherperson—may or may not, in fact, have a clear mental picture of what the hell a midge even is—but the report will be accurate.

"Exactly *where* are they getting them on midges?" you ask.

———

South Platte River, Colorado: It is a promisingly warm April night. You sit at the flytying desk faced with a small pile of #18 dry fly hooks and a much larger pile of materials in natural dun and shades of dyed olive. To your right, next to the cup of coffee, sits a fly box that has been nearly picked clean by the Blue-winged Olive hatch on the South Platte—last fall's hatch, and the one that is going on right now, the one you fished three days ago and will drive down to hit again tomorrow morning.

When you think "Platte" you picture the first clear view of the river from the trail: the shot nearly straight down into the glassy Ice Box Pool with the huge gray boulders at its head looking like, as Dave Taylor of Trout Unlimited says, "elephants on a skating rink." In the right light you can see the trout stacked in there. Lots of them. Big ones. They're either rising to some tiny hatch or nymphing. They look easy, but they are not.

You're not thinking of the fish you caught the other day, but the ones you didn't, especially the one in the backwater under the big, flat rock decorated with the stripes of high-water marks. He wouldn't even look at the Olive Dun Quill, then glanced at the no-hackle and the Paradun, seemed to actually sniff at the floating nymph, and then just dissolved away, leaving the last of the hatch to a smaller trout.

Under the fly-fisher's kinky, existential scoring system, a fish like that cancels out dozens that were hooked and landed.

Maybe a quill-bodied no-hackle, or a trailing husk, upright-winged emerger, or perhaps a split-winged dry fly with a parachute hackle tied underneath the body. It's late, and a full night's sleep would feel good in the morning, but what you really need is something just a little bit different than all the Blue-winged Olives that rainbow has already seen.

—

Gunnison River, Colorado: You are lying under a juniper tree in an unzipped down sleeping bag in the Gunnison Gorge, one day out on the float trip. Already you're used to feeling closed in by the high canyon walls. Even now, in low late summer flow, this is a big river in a small space. In most places there is no way out except impossibly straight up toward the slot of blue sky or on downriver the way you're going. In a very palpable way, there is noplace else, just this. To get the same isolation on flat ground you'd have to go north until you hit tundra.

The night is warm, the moon is up, and there are only a few mosquitoes. From the absence of grunts and rustles in the other bags scattered around, you guess that the rest of the party is asleep.

Except for Tom Austin, that is. As we were all drifting away from the fire, looking for a spot to lie down on that was level and free of ants, Tom was stringing up a rod and tying on an enormous rabbit hair sculpin. You sensed that the head guide was not entirely happy about that, although he knew enough not to say anything discouraging to a guy who is Going Night Fishing in a big way.

Guides are like mother ducks: they like to have everyone accounted for at all times.

So maybe you're not the only one lying awake listening to the river, waiting for footsteps to come up out of it. Go to sleep, you tell yourself; if he gets one on that huge streamer, he'll wake you up and tell you all about it.

———

Roaring Fork of the Colorado: You're fishing a golden stonefly nymph in that deep plunge pool at the head of the long run, the one that takes six split shot to get to the bottom of, even now when the water is low. It has been a slow day, with nothing but whitefish so far, and you find yourself wishing once again that you were one of those guys who know the Roaring Fork; who know, for instance, where the big trout are.

Then you tell yourself that whitefish are better than no fish at all, that they are perfectly honorable when caught on flies, which is true enough, and you begin to fish a little more casually. It's not always going to be like the cover of a glossy magazine, right?

The river here seems bigger than it is because it tugs at you so insistently. This water falls a long way from the headwaters down to the Colorado River. It seems to be in a hurry to get there; things happen quickly, and there are a lot of places it won't let you go. They don't call it the Roaring Fork for nothing.

You've fished this stretch maybe twenty times over the years and have never even tried to get to the other side. The other side, of course, looks pretty damned good.

The next strike doesn't crank you up too much until you feel the weight. In fact, that throbbing could be nothing but the current working against a snagged leader. But then there is the unmistakable shaking of a big head down there.

Oh, shit.

The fish turns, heads down into the run where the water gets white, staying deep. You feel the leader ticking and bumping against all kinds of junk on the bottom, and then you're standing there like an idiot holding a slack line.

Surely it was just another whitefish—a big mother, sure, but still just a whitefish.

———

Green River, Utah: Little two-lane Highway 6 out of Golden to I-70 West, and then halfway across Colorado on four lanes at high speeds in the general direction of Utah. North at the town of Rifle (after a stop to fill the thermos) and up to Meeker where you turn west again along the White River. Coming down out of the Flattops onto rolling high plains, the river here is wide, muddy, and full of carp. With those flat, lava mountains to the east, you are suddenly in unexplored territory, sitting up a little straighter on the truck seat.

At this moment in your life you have only heard of the Green where it's a fast, cold stream in the tall canyon under the dam. They say it's like so many other trout rivers you'll probably know what to do, but it's still going to be a new one.

You know vaguely that farther down the land folds open, and the stream gets wider and warmer until eventually it becomes a high desert river that has unearthed many fossils. Maybe there are big brown trout down there, and maybe not. Certainly there are rattlesnakes. The downriver reports have been secondhand, conflicting and tantalizing. Someday you may have to go look at that, too (on a long drive your mind spreads in this kind of widening circle), but right now it's off your personal map, so it might as well be filled with perpetual fog and monsters.

Coming up on Dinosaur, Colorado—just minutes from the Utah border—you stop for some pop and a look under the hood of the truck. It's running okay at cruising speeds, but is stalling when you slow down. Nothing is obviously amiss, but then neither of you is what could be called a mechanic.

The decision is obvious: if it cruises okay, then let's cruise. If it stalls when you slow down, then don't slow down.

At the junction of Highways 40 and 64 stands a snarling green plaster dinosaur in need of paint. Heat is rippling in the air, so you can't quite focus on it. The day has shaped up prickly hot, sage-scented, and a little dusty, even without wind, and you would feel depressingly far from any trout except for the Uinta Mountains standing on the western horizon. Down here the white stuff is alkali. Up ahead it's snow.

———

Bitterroot River, Montana: The guy at the fly shop, standing under a sign that reads BITTERROOT TROUT DON'T SPEAK LATIN, said you only need one fly, an Ugly Radimus. "Well, then, what are all these other flies for?" you asked, pointing at the bins of hoppers, mayflies, and caddis patterns. The answer was vague, something to do with tourists and hedged bets.

So the four of you hit the river armed with several dozen Ugly Radimuses (or is it "Radimi"?) and, sure enough, the fish like them, at least for a while. When the Red Quill hatch comes off, the fish, not surprisingly, want a Red Quill, size 14, but after that it's the Radimus again, in the fast water and along the banks.

Okay, it's the only fly you need *between hatches*. Fair enough.

You're high up on the Bitterroot's main branch, above the last bridge where boats put in, just below the confluence of the East and West forks. These are almost the headwaters, the place where the Bitterroot Range of mountains come south, jog north, then swing south again, surrounding you in a rough, three-sided bowl that the river flows out of going north. There's no one around.

The river is fast here, running only in the deepest channel in the fast spots, and then spreading out in the riffles, but you can see from the wide streambed where it gets a lot bigger in the spring.

Right through here it seems to be full of rainbows and cutthroats all the way from fifteen inches to little finger-sized ones with parr marks. This is exactly the spot where what you'd call a mountain stream becomes what you'd call a river.

Later in the afternoon you meet another fisherman. He's crouching on a glistening white stretch of exposed sand and round, bleached river rocks examining a bear track. "Is that a grizzly?" he asks, and you say, "Too small, probably a black."

From that he takes you to be a local, and asks what kind of cutthroats these are. "West slope," you say, having learned that just this morning.

Then he looks at the fly in your hook keeper and says, "Now, is that an Ugly Radimus or a Madam X?"

"Don't know for sure," you say, "we don't get that technical around here."

———

Yellowstone River: After your first day on the Yellowstone at Buffalo Ford, you find that you have been infested with buffalo mites. It's not a pleasant experience, but, it occurs to you, it is a singular distinction in this day and age. A.K. leans over, sniffs at your shirt, and says, "Well, the bugs made an honest mistake. You smell like a bison in rut."

Just a few miles downstream from its source at Yellowstone Lake, the river here is already wide, deep, big, and western. Fishermen work it close to the banks because that's about all you can do. Luckily, that's also where the fish are. The Ford is the only place around here where man or beast can cross. Sometimes the man will have a little trouble with the current.

It's a toss-up which you were more impressed with, the pretty cutthroats or the buffalo, although it's the latter that are statistically more dangerous than the grizzly bears. That's because they stand around looking prehistoric but peaceful, and people think they can pet them, or put their kids on their backs for pictures. Nine times out of ten, they're dead wrong about that.

At one of the usual buffalo traffic jams, tourist after tourist, each with an Instamatic camera, gets too close, and a harried ranger yells at them. Another ranger comes over to your car and asks if you've seen a guy he's looking for, a guy who, according to amazed witnesses, jumped on a bull buffalo, rode him fifty yards across a meadow, and then stepped off neatly to scattered applause.

"That's a real no-no," the ranger says.

You haven't seen him, but you'll look. The guy was described as weighing two hundred pounds, wearing a denim jacket with the sleeves cut off, and riding a Harley.

"If we spot him," you say, "we'll grab him for you."

CHAPTER 14

A Quiet Week

(WITH APOLOGIES TO GARRISON KEILLOR)

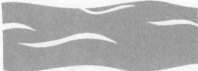

It has been a quiet week in East Big Fish. Lance, the owner of the Pompous Angler Fly Shop, was over at the Cafe Eat the other morning with his wife, Muffy. They were having dry whole wheat toast and herbal tea, as usual, and Lance seemed to be in sort of a poor mood. He even got a little short with Agnes when she kidded him about how maybe he wouldn't be as sour in the mornings if he started eating a man's breakfast like the rest of the boys.

Agnes really was kidding, too. I mean, she started serving that herbal tea because Lance and Muffy, and some of their customers, had asked for it in the first place. If Lance had said what he'd said ("Why don't you mind your own business?") with one eye closed and a half smile on his face as others at the Cafe Eat do, it would have been okay. But he didn't.

When Agnes brought their tea, you could hear the saucers hit the table from out in the parking lot.

Lance was depressed because, as he'd mentioned the day before, and the day before that, the out-of-state fishermen were going to other rivers—and, presumably, other fly shops—because the hatches there were on time, while here the *Ephemerella infrequens* had come off before the season even opened and now the *Ephemerella doddsi* were late.

I overheard that from a nearby table where I was sitting with Harvey, of Harvey's Gas Worms Cold Beer Groceries and Fishing Tackle. He leaned over and said to me, in an informative tone, "I think he's referring to the fact that the fish ain't been biting lately." Harvey has been in the tackle business for forty-three years and likes to help clear things up when the talk gets overly technical.

We're a trout fishing town here, all 427 year-around residents, so café discussions of how the fishing has been are a little more serious than they are in some other places. When Harvey finally told Agnes what Lance was upset about, she forgave him—she hadn't realized it was so serious—although she continues to insist that a few cups of regular old hot coffee in the morning would do his disposition a world of good.

Directly or indirectly, just about everything here depends on the fishing. There's the K.O.A. Campground and the Brown Trout Guest Cabins north of town and, in the downtown business loop itself, there's Harvey's Gas Worms, etc., the relatively new Pompous Angler, and the much older Bob's Flies and Guide Service, not to mention the town's two dining establishments, the Cafe Eat and the Roundup Cafe, plus the Branding Iron Bar and the Suds-N-Duds Laundromat. All of these places have stuffed trout on their walls (even the Laundromat) and are patronized heavily by fishermen in season (even the Laundromat) and probably wouldn't survive otherwise.

If you don't own or work in one of these places, guide, or tie flies, you either get bused into the county seat to school or just hang around home all day. Whatever you do, you know what everyone else does and you know how the fishing has been lately.

It's a typical small town in that if you were born here or are only here for a week of fishing, you're welcome. But if you move here from somewhere else you're viewed with considerable suspicion.

Lance and Muffy found that out when they opened the new fly shop which, being of the Swiss chalet persuasion, stands out on Main Street like a flying saucer and made a lot of people uneasy at first. Not the least of them was Bob, who said publicly that any idiot could see there was only enough business for one fly shop and there was already one here. And, he added, it had been here for two generations. As any resident of any small tourist community knows, the scale of time that really counts is measured in generations. Everything else is just dust in the wind.

Harvey was neutral, since he also sells food and gas and his fishing tackle consists largely of salmon eggs, garlic-flavored marshmallows, and worms.

Through that first fishing season, Bob would not actually speak to Lance, although when he ran into him he'd nod and grunt in the interest of civility. But then it began to look like there was enough business to go around.

For one thing, the locals who didn't use worms went to Bob's because they'd always gone there, even back when Bob himself was in high school and guiding for his dad in the summers. And most of the old customers—after a quick stop at the Pompous Angler just to look around—came back, too. Fishermen are a fickle bunch, but once they hit middle age they do seem to develop some loyalties. Either that, or they're just too stubborn and set in their ways to change.

After a while we began to notice a distinct difference between the clientele of the two shops: Bob got the older guys driving American pickups and wearing canvas chest waders and floppy hats. And no women to speak of. Lance's customers were some younger, drove cars (often foreign), and wore skintight neoprene waders and caps. Many were accompanied by wives or lady friends dressed pretty much the same way.

Eventually it got to where we could sit around the café and tell who was shopping at which fly store. Aside from their general appearance, Lance's customers asked about the "no smoking" section (there isn't one) and talked earnestly about hatches and spinner falls using lots of Latin terminology. A lot of the guys from Bob's smoked pipes and spoke more casually of Royal Wulffs and Hares Ears. And anyway, many of the latter looked familiar, that is, if not the individuals, then at least the type.

Agnes—who had begun to sell the hell out of herbal tea and bran muffins—was one of the early peacemakers, urging Bob to "live and let live" in the fly shop department. And Bob did, finally.

It happened in the second season after Lance arrived. A couple of young guys from New York came in and asked if the *Ptaronarcys californicus* had begun to emerge yet and, although Bob could easily have translated that into black stone fly, he said, "Maybe you ought to go ask Lance about that."

It turned out to be a good move all around. The guys bought their licenses and flies from Lance, but then came back to Bob's saying, "His guides were all booked, but he said you had some funky old wooden mack boats and good local guides."

Funky? Bob thought.

Lance's boats are bright yellow, fiberglass, and up until that moment Bob had been a little jealous. In fact, one night at the Branding Iron, right after the Pompous Angler opened, Bob had a few too many beers and admitted to feeling a little old and worn out lately, pointing out that he was fifty-two and no kid anymore, and couldn't afford a whole fleet of new boats like "some people."

But the two guys from New York seemed to kind of turn him around on that. He guided them himself because all his regular guides were already out. They caught lots of big trout, some on the entomologically correct *Pteronarcys* nymphs Lance had sold them, but most on Bob's Black Uglies, which are a local variation of the Wooly Worm.

Later the two sports bragged about the neat old guide they'd found with a few missing teeth, a slow, casual pace, and corny good humor who got them into more trout than they'd seen before in their collective lifetimes. They'd called him "Sir" for a while until Bob told them to cut it out.

After that Bob took to wearing his cowboy hat again and began doing more trips himself. He lost a little weight, too, and got a nice tan. He never talked about it, but if I had to guess I'd say he stopped feeling old and started feeling venerable; a fine distinction, but an important one. Young people calling you "Sir" can do that.

And, for that matter, after a couple of seasons Lance's chamois shirts faded, lost their nap, and got threadbare at the elbows—from rowing, some said, while others claimed it was from leaning on the counter. His beard went gradually from professorial to just country, and he started stocking Bob's Uglies in the shop.

Then, just last summer, a famous fishing writer came to town and drove straight to Lance's shop where he parked his Land Rover under the big molded plastic mayfly sign that said OPEN. After carefully writing down all the best hatches and all the best times of year to fish, he asked about the history of the river, and Lance said, "Bob's the one who can tell you about that. He was born here."

Lance walked the writer the two blocks over to Bob's shop and introduced him in such a way that if Bob had never heard of the guy, he'd at least understand that he should have. The three of them ended up having lunch together at the Cafe Eat (the meat loaf special) and then they all went fishing. Bob and Lance took the writer to the best spots, got him into lots of trout, and sent him home with fifteen rolls of exposed film, pages of notes, and stars in his eyes. Then Bob and Lance went and had a drink together.

Bob said, "Shoot, that guy could hardly fish, and you say he's famous?"

"He is famous," Lance said.

"Well," Bob replied, "you're a better fisherman than he is."

That was a left-handed compliment, but it was the best Bob could do. Lance figured it was good enough.

———

It took the better part of five years, but Lance and Muffy are now widely considered to be residents, although only their children will be seen as legitimate East Big Fishers. It helped a lot that they spend the winters here. If you don't spend the winters here, you are from wherever you *do* spend them.

The feud which, looking back on it now, didn't really amount to much, probably helped, too. Making peace with someone tends to bring them into the fold, but before you can make peace, you have to have a little war. The other day when Muffy came into the café complaining about a couple of idiot tourists, everyone sympathized without a trace of irony.

"I wish they'd just go back where they came from," Muffy said, and Bob replied from a neighboring table, "That's the nice part about it, honey. Sooner or later they all do."

Muffy has pretty much stopped bristling at being called "Honey."

———

The river flows under the two-lane bridge down at the end of Main Street. It's a decent trout river for its size; not the best in the state, but not too many notches down from the top either. You'll read about it now and then in what Lance calls "the literature." It's pretty slow through here with some long riffles—nothing you could call rapids even at high water—and lots of good, braided dry fly water. It's plenty big enough to float, but small enough to wade, too, and you can fish it nicely either way.

And it's a beautiful river, even to those of us who have seen it every day of our lives, and so don't even really look at the thing for weeks on end.

There are some fine hatches, but it can be moody, which is why most of us locals, following Bob's lead, fish it with nymphs. You can almost always get 'em on nymphs. We tend to find a hole and fish the hell out of it while the drift boats shoot past. Sometimes the fancy sports look down their noses at us as if we didn't really belong here, even though it is, of course, the other way around.

Lance, on the other hand, is a dry fly fisherman. He carries five times the number of flies any of us do and covers that much more water in a day's fishing. He's a pretty caster to watch and even Bob allows as how the guy can catch a lot of fish.

If you asked anyone on the street, they'd tell you that Lance catches more trout, but Bob catches more *big* trout; and also that Bob does best in higher water, while Lance really comes into his own in the lower flows of late summer and fall. It's a kind of natural division of labor with a changing of the guard sometime in late July or early August.

The tourist fishermen begin to arrive about the time the river comes down from the spring runoff and the early hatches start. Some are wide-eyed and excited—mostly the young ones who have read about our river here in magazines and books and have finally made the pilgrimage. The older guys tend to be a little slower and more businesslike, but they're excited, too, having learned on many past vacations just how good the river can be if you have the patience to wait it out.

The old hands know that Bob's guides are the ones to hire early in the season because they're a bit older, live here year around, and have had the chance to scope the water out before the season started. Lance's guides are college kids who have only been in town for a week before their first trips. Even the local kids haven't really checked out the river; they've been too busy looking up old sweethearts and boozing it up with old pals. They are young, strong, enthusiastic, and good boatmen. They're the best to hire later in the season when things get hot and heavy.

By the middle of summer the town is packed with fly-fishermen. Most live in campers or tents, either at the K.O.A. or at one of the Forest Service campgrounds, but the Brown Trout Guest Cabins are full all summer long, too. Both cafés serve fishermen's specials and, although the Suds-N-Duds isn't exactly crowded, it gets used. Sam, the owner, says the dryers see more action than the washing machines.

We're a few miles off the main highway here, so there's hardly any traffic except for mornings and evenings, and then you see cars with license plates from all over the country and pickup trucks towing mack boats to put-in and take-out points along the river.

Harvey's Gas Worms Cold Beer Groceries and Fishing Tackle always does a good business, although Harvey himself tends to deny it. I mean, everyone either staying in town or passing through needs or wants at least one of the aforementioned items, and since Harvey's is the only store worthy of the name for sixteen miles in one direction and thirty-one in the other, he can charge pretty much what he wants—which is a lot.

Harvey also sells a lot of worms, so many that the van from Merl's Worm Ranch shows up twice a week to fill the cooler with fresh ones. Some think that's odd, since the river right through here is catch-and-release, flies only now. But Harvey knows there are lots of other places to fish, like the reservoir, some lakes, and a couple of small streams, where people can use bait and kill fish like the Good Lord intended. Harvey has nothing against fly-fishermen, although he thinks some of them are way too serious about it, but he does have something against catch-and-release regulations.

"It just ain't natural," he sometimes observes.

Harvey is something of an expert on worms, although no one around here can remember the last time he actually went fishing. You tell him where you're going, and he'll recommend red worms, crawlers, or Georgia jumpers.

Lance naturally thinks the no-kill rule is great and wouldn't have started his shop here without it.

It's Bob who's neutral on this one. He knows it's good for business in at least two ways: it keeps fish in the river (and Bob knows that a river can get fished out, he's seen it happen) and it also attracts a certain class of fishermen, namely guys who are willing to spend money and who don't choke at $1.50 for a dry fly.

Still, he remembers the days when catch-and-release regulations weren't *necessary* and sort of misses them. He misses the fish fries out on the sandbars in the evenings, and the guys who used to come in to show him a big, dripping stringer of trout they'd killed using his nymphs. A few times a year someone would come in with a real pig, and ask about a taxidermist.

The most recent mount on his wall is a lovely, fat, four-pound brook trout that was killed in a nearby pond, but most of the others came from the river. The biggest, a sixteen-pound,

four-ounce brown, was taken in 1957. It's a pretty mount, but it's
beginning to look a little ratty, and the guy who caught the fish
is dead. Bob sometimes looks at it and thinks, Anyone can have
a hog trout from thirty years ago.

But from his newfound vantage point as the gray-haired,
fly-fishing sage of East Big Fish, he is philosophical. "Well," he
says, "things change."

Things do change. The fishing is still as good as it ever was,
but it's harder now and it seems as if there are more fly-
fishermen every season. Most of us who actually live here don't
fish the river much until late in the year when the weather gets
unpredictable and the crowd thins out some. We fish the lakes
and streams and do pretty well for ourselves, though. It would
be nice to be able to get on the river more, and we sometimes
complain about it, but we know that without all these people
around here for four or five months out of the year, the place
would probably dry up and blow away.

I guess we have one of those love/hate things with the tourists,
but, whatever else they're like, they're on a fishing trip and
they're happy. It's hard to hold that against anyone.

I guess what I'm trying to say is, we mostly love 'em more
than we hate 'em.

Speaking of tourists, Harvey started renting videotapes this
year. He did that at the insistence of his wife, Ethel, who said it
was something city people expected now. So above the weathered wooden sign proclaiming Gas Worms Cold Beer Groceries
and Fishing Tackle, they added a red-and-yellow plastic one
that flashes off and on and says VIDEO MANIA PIT STOP. They even
tumbled for a small adult section (something else city people
expect), and one night, after reading the titles and looking at the
covers, they decided to take a VCR home and watch a few, just
to make sure they weren't too awful to have in the store.

Ten minutes into the first one, Ethel said to Harvey, "You can
watch this foolishness of you want to. I'm going to bed." Which she
did, taking more time at it and making more noise than usual.

When she got up at six the next morning, Harvey was still in
front of the TV watching *Leather Hospital* in which these two
young nurses were . . . Well, never mind.

She said she was ashamed of him, but she wasn't. I mean, you keep your mouth shut about the things you're really ashamed of, and Ethel ended up telling everyone in town and half her customers about it over the next week. It came out as a complaint, but I thought she was actually proud of Harvey for still being that frisky at his age. When I mentioned that to her one day, she came dangerously close to smiling and said, "Well, at least he didn't take the VCR apart to see how it worked."

Whenever this came up Harvey would always quickly change the subject by saying, "Sure, I looked at a couple of them, but mostly I was watching those Masters Series tapes on fly-fishing. The trout are bitin' now, by the way. The *Ephemerella doddsi* hatch was late this year, but they started coming off just the other day. It's been real good."

And it *has* been good. The first day the bugs came off there was almost no one in town and me and some of the boys had the Bend Pool and most of the meadow stretch all to ourselves. Trout were rising everywhere, so we fished dry flies. And yes, we already had some in our boxes. We're not hicks, you know.

Now, after only two or three days, the word has spread and every guide in town is working. There seem to be more strange faces than usual rowing the boats this year.

Many of the guides are still college kids, but fewer and fewer of them are from here. A lot of our kids go off to college now swearing they'll never come back and, sure enough, don't, except for the odd Christmas or family funeral. We hear how their lives are going, but we don't really know what *happens* to them the way we'd know if they stayed around here.

Oh, sure, we know in a general way that they get caught up in another kind of life. Hell, some of them get caught up in that while they're still here, which accounts for, among other things, the occasional tart whiff of marijuana you'll sometimes walk into on Main Street on a warm summer evening. We know it's the kind of life you eventually have to get away from by going someplace—like here, for instance—to fly-fish for trout for a few weeks. The kind of life where "How's the fishing?" is considered to be idle chatter.

CHAPTER 15

WYOMING

 My old Courtland landing net, the one I carried on fishing trips for years, is now lying somewhere in the upper North Platte River Valley in southern Wyoming. With any luck, it's been picked up by another fisherman and is now in use, though probably it's waterlogged and rotting on the bottom of the pond. That is, I think that's where it ended up. When something is lost you're never exactly sure where it is or it wouldn't really be lost, right?

By way of consolation, a friend told me that if you go off and leave something behind, it means you have a serious need to go back to the place where you left it. Not to find the thing in question, mind you. We're talking mystical reasons here, some form of spiritual gravity.

Okay, fine, I'm not immune to cosmic influences, but I don't like losing things. Gear is expendable, but it should be used up and thrown away, not left behind by accident.

And I still needed a net. I have a spare, but it's one of those little bitty ones that were fashionable a few years ago; you know, the ones that were light and easy to handle, but too small for any fish that actually required a net to land.

The trip I'd just come back from had firmly reminded me that

there are times when a guy needs a nice, big net, so I drove into
the Front Range Angler fly shop in Boulder to buy a new one.

"New net, eh?"

"Yeah, lost the old one in Wyoming."

"I'll bet there's a story there."

"No story. I just lost my fucking net, okay?"

The new one is a big, wide-mouthed Broden made of zebra
wood and ash. It's very pretty, and a little on the expensive side,
but what the hell. I always wanted a Broden, so I wrote it off as
a case of forced upgrading, and made a vow to try and hold onto
it.

Losing the net on that trip was appropriate, I guess, because
Wyoming fits into my personal mythology as the kind of place
that can swallow things up without a trace—single engine airplanes, pickup trucks, people, landing nets, you name it. The
very sound of the words, "lost in Wyoming" have a doomed ring
to them, as if the thing in question wouldn't be any more
irretrievable if it were on the dark side of the moon.

Many of my friends and I have a way of neglecting Wyoming.
When you live in Northern Colorado, Wyoming can become
nothing more than that big flat thing you have to drive across to
get to Idaho and Montana. North to south, it's roughly ten hours
tall. For reasons I've never been able to determine, it can be an
hour longer on the way back. Either way, it's a grind.

I've been on many drives like that over the years. The ones
where you ride silently through that long stretch where no radio
stations reach—silently because you're hours into the trip and
have already talked everything out at least once. No music, no
conversation. You gaze through the windshield in a kind of
trance until finally your passenger points out the window, and
says with genuine excitement, "Look, a tree!"

That's in vehicles of the old school with nothing but a radio.
More recently I've made the trek armed with a tape deck, and
now Wyoming has much to do with traveling at high speeds
listening to rock and roll at equally high volumes to cut through
the shrieking of the wind.

Depending on the company, that is. If I'm with Jim Pruett it might be reggae, or Paul Winter space jazz. The latter I find a bit too cerebral for the excessive speeds you reach on those long straight highways, and the album recorded in the Taj Mahal has parts in it that sound like a loose bearing in the water pump.

In the back of one's mind there is always the creeping horror of blowing a water pump seventy-five miles out of Rock Springs.

Sure, I know there are mountains and rivers up there—I've seen them from a distance, and even been in them a time or two—but the parts you have to gut your way across are the archetypal wide-open spaces with horizon-to-horizon sagebrush relieved only by the receding ribbon of highway under you and the occasional lonesome cow.

Not that I'm exactly complaining. I still prefer the folded geography of mountains, or at least the shelter of trees, but, after over twenty years of living in the West, I've come to appreciate the plains. Too much of it can give you the prairie madness, but in small doses it's good for you. It's an acquired taste.

Not long ago the state of Wyoming announced that it wanted to attract some artists and writers to give the place a little more of a cultural ambience. It was a great deal for thoughtful types, they said. Cheap living, few distractions, and lots of peace and quiet.

That's for sure.

I thought of that the morning of the day the net turned up missing, while gazing out through the open door of an outhouse at a neatly framed piece of Wyoming. The scene was downright Oriental in its simplicity: bluish-gray sky, greenish-gray sage, and a gopher. No snowcapped mountains, no sentimental pines. It was refreshing.

I had tried to paint years ago in the Midwest, but it didn't work out, and I ended up a writer instead. Looking back on it I think it was the preponderance of objects in any given composition. Too much stuff, too many brushstrokes, at a time when I wanted simplicity. Painting hadn't occurred to me in a long time, but there, in that part of Wyoming where daily life goes on just a peg or two above sensory deprivation, I think I could do it. And I'd save a bundle on art supplies, too.

It was an idle thought at dawn, a time when there were fish to be caught.

I was up there with my friend Jay Allman, fishing a working ranch where he and a handful of others lease the fishing rights to several fine prairie ponds. Jay is the owner of Trout Traps, Ltd., the float tube manufacturers. I guess he'd qualify as an executive, though you wouldn't pick him out of a crowd as such in his cowboy hat and T-shirt.

Jay refers to the ranch as the Official Trout Traps Belly Boat Field Testing Facility. The Branch Office consists of a small, somewhat battered trailer with a propane stove, but no electricity, and an outhouse with an uncluttered view and several .30 caliber bullet holes in it. Plugging crappers is considered a respectable sport here in the West—with a year-around open season. Spend enough time on the plains and you'll begin to see the charm of it.

The trailer sits on the banks of the largest pond—more of a lake, really—with the trailers of a few other leasors in sight. Most of them are bigger and prettier than Jay's, including a couple of shiny Air Streams, but Jay is not the kind of guy to squander a lot of money on something so basic as shelter. An aluminum rowboat with trolling motor is tied up three steps from the front door. This is no-frills country living at its best.

The ponds are very rich, but deceptively plain-looking. At first glance they look like they should hold bass and bluegills, if anything at all, but no. It's trout. Big trout.

Jay says the quality of the ponds has to do in part with the sagebrush depositing calcium in the soil that then leaches into the water to beef up the chemistry. If you're not already familiar with the place, I can't begin to tell you how much sage there is in Wyoming.

The ponds are thick with vegetation, and, because they are cool, but lying in the relatively low band of high plains habitat, they carry a diverse mix of aquatic food forms, all in large populations. There are scuds so thick you have to wash them from your waders when you come out of the water; warm-water creatures like damsel and dragonflies; and cold-water ones like various mayflies and caddis. The picture you get of the trout in ponds like these is that they could never really be hungry. They have the freshwater shrimp to graze on more or less constantly, and they seem to suck up the other bugs more for variety than anything else. If they're not lazy, they are certainly contented.

The centerpiece hatch is the ubiquitous monster prairie lake caddis, a wheat-colored bug about an inch and a half long that lives in every good prairie lake or pond I've ever fished. It's the still-water equivalent of the great western stone fly, though it's not nearly as well known.

———

This had started out as a desperation fishing trip, one that had fallen through a time or two already that summer, but that we both felt we needed badly. Like most executive types, Jay works way too long and hard for his own good. Like many writers, I don't work nearly as hard as I claim to, but still somehow manage to suffer from periods of seemingly job-related burnout. Jay needed to get back to his ponds, and had been trying to do so for the better part of a month. I felt I needed to accomplish a little stress management, and also wanted to see if half of what he'd said about this place was true.

Finally there was the phone call:

"Meet me at seven Tuesday morning. I am getting the hell out of here."

I was typing. A deadline was coming up.

"I'll be there," I said.

Tuesday had a lot to do with high speeds and Led Zeppelin ("Stairway to Heaven" is still a great song), and I was scribbling in one of the notebooks the newspaper gives me that says NEWS—PROFESSIONAL REPORTER'S NOTEBOOK. Yes, that's a little pompous, but they're free. Still, we were at the ranch, unpacked and rigged up, long before the evening rise on the big pond. I felt fresh, but wobbly, as if we'd stopped too quickly. Wyoming is not nearly so formidable when it's where you're going.

Late that afternoon we putted across the pond in the boat to fish by wading the far shore. My first trout, a little ten-inch brown, hooked himself as I was impatiently stripping in a bad cast for another try. This doesn't quite qualify as catching a fish by mistake—I mean, you *are* fishing, after all—but it's not what you'd call a fine job of trout angling either.

Jay had suggested streamers until things picked up, so I'd tied on an all-purpose olive-colored Weedless Wooly, and was practicing my distance cast. I'm not too bad at this as long as real tournament ranges aren't called for, but when I haven't been on still water for a while it takes me a good twenty minutes to work into it.

For that matter, it can take me a little while to get into just plain fishing itself when things back in the world have been hectic. My pace is wrong, and there are all these things in my head, including the lead guitar part from a certain Led Zeppelin tune.

Working on the long cast is a good beginning. With all that line in the air you have to tell yourself, Sloooooow down on the backcast. What's the rush? Dad used to ask me that when I was a teenager. "What's the rush?" It's as fair a question now as it was then, and it always seems to come in his tone of honest curiosity. Like if there was a good reason, then okay.

And don't put your shoulder into a distance cast, you think. You've been doing this long enough to know it's not a matter of brute force. This expensive bamboo fly rod with the nickel silver fittings is here to work, you are here to orchestrate.

Jay, of course, was casting beautifully right off the bat in that crisp, businesslike way that graphite rod fishermen have. And this after checking in at the factory that morning, and then driving for five hours in a souped-up Blazer, screaming snatches of conversation over a howling electric guitar. But then, he's in a different line of work.

In a technical sense, the cast is the soul of fly-fishing. When you have it down, you're there. In a nontechnical sense, you can then begin to consider where "there" is.

In this case, it was the valley of the North Platte River: the thin strip of riparian habitat along the stream itself, with high plains on either side of that, and the beginnings of forested foothills beyond *that*. The ponds were in the open, low-lying dishes tucked into miles and miles of sage, but from just about any of them you could spot hills and some trees if you started to get a little agoraphobic. Farther to the west are the Sierra Madre Mountains, to the east the Medicine Bows. It's classic western ranchland—prairie with water—and mercifully far from the interstate highways.

—

Jay had told me how good this water was, and I believed him without reservation. We have one of those unspoken treaties that would go something like, "I'm too good a fisherman to lie, and you're too good to believe me anyway." Still, the first night at a new place breeds misgivings. With coaching, you know what to expect, but in another just as real way, you have no *idea* what to expect. At first the big pond lay there, glassy and ordinary-looking, except that this was known to be fine trout water. The effect is not unlike seeing a sports car crouched under a canvas tarp.

The first few trout were small, and came from the weedy shallows on our side of the drop-off. I'd released my first one with some impatience, but by the time I hooked the second the cast was working more smoothly, and I took a minute to look at him. A foot long, nicely colored, healthy, little teeth, staring eye: a regulation, pan-sized brown trout, but, nonetheless, a new fish from new water. And you can't have big trout without some little ones.

Not long after the sun went off the pond, the first boils appeared predictably over the deeper water, and I experienced that psychological squaring of the shoulders—the old, "Okay, here we go, better evaluate the situation."

The specks in the air, on closer inspection, turned out to be gangly, long-legged midges looking like mosquitoes, but without the little hypodermic syringes. The slightly larger check marks on the surface were Callibaetis mayfly duns with the particular mottled markings on the wings that would key them out—if one cared to go through that agony rather than fish—as one of the twenty-some species of this bug.

And the caddis were just caddis, big enough to pick out clearly even at some distance. They were also what the fish were eating.

I'd tied up some of these large bugs with quill wings and sparse hackles for still water, but it had turned out that they didn't float well. Fly tying lesson #248: a size 6 dry fly can't be dressed as lightly, relative to hook size, as a size 14. There's too much steel in the hook, too much weight for the surface tension.

Then again, these things would float for a cast or two if you didn't skate them, and once under the surface they made a fair emerger. Lesson #249: don't throw the flies away too soon.

After a dozen or so casts with the caddis, I snapped the fly off in a fish that left a loud, flushing boil behind it, the kind of cold-water shark that forces the smaller fish to feed shyly somewhere else, giving the impression that there *are* no little fish. I nicked two more very large trout, but lost them, and finally retrieved the fly and sharpened the hook. Then I popped the fly off in a fourth trout by setting up entirely too hard on the strike.

I was getting pretty excited, which is something you don't actually have to do. When fishing writers describe the circus atmosphere of a good rise, they are mostly putting their own emotions onto the trout. You don't have to be cold-blooded to be a good fly-fisherman, but there are times when you need to remain calm. It sometimes works to just watch for a few minutes, perhaps breathing deeply and slowly at the same time.

Okay, in reality, trout weighing several pounds eating large flies is a perfectly ordinary circumstance here. It probably happened last night, it will just as probably happen tomorrow night, and after you've packed up and left, too. It's business as usual.

Since I'd looked last the sky had gotten purple. A great blue heron was flapping slowly off to the west, long neck tucked up,

legs trailing behind him sentimentally. Nothing out of the
ordinary.

I retied the leader with a heavier tippet, knotted on a new fly,
and methodically sharpened the hook to a needle point. Okay.
Then I looked up to see that the bugs were gone and the rise was
over, just like that. That purring, splashing sound was Jay
reeling in and wading back toward the boat.

———

The next morning we loaded the belly boats into the truck,
and drove back up the road a mile to Jay's favorite pond. It was
a small one, the kind where fishing from a float tube gives you
a feeling of omnipotence. It was kidney-shaped, deep in the
middle, and had a mucky bottom with lots of weeds. There were
stands of cattails along the inside curve of the bank, and a long
inlet arm snaking off to the south. Along the north end was a
muddy slide where the cattle waded in to drink. All in all it was
your standard stock pond, except that a little after dawn there
were big trout charging around in it, leaving their wakes and
swirls on the surface.

That morning Jay had said that if there were damselfly
nymphs in the water to use my best copy, otherwise use a leech.

"How about the big caddis?" I asked, always wanting to fish
the dry fly.

"Maybe tonight," Jay said, slamming the truck a little too
quickly over the washed-out clay road leading to the pond.

Wild stories and predictions are what you usually hear on the
way to someone's favorite water. Jay said very little, but was
clearly in a big hurry to get there. There was no rock and roll
now, though. Now it was just grinding gears and meadowlarks.

Ten feet into the shallow end of the pond, I looked down and
saw the pale green, inch-long damsel nymphs in the water.
Herds of them were migrating to the weeds where they could
crawl out and hatch into flies. Some were climbing onto the float
tube with me. They were all action, wiggling frantically, and
making as much headway side to side as forward, sort of like a
chubby old house cat trying to run.

It was too shallow yet to use the flippers properly, so I was pushing with my heels, kicking up billows of mud, and tying on a damsel fly nymph.

My damsel nymph is pretty basic for this day and age: thin-bodied with a wisp of marabou at the tail, bluish-green pheasant hackle, and—the one concession to snazziness—black painted bead chain eyeballs that are so easy I couldn't resist. People have sometimes admired them, which is often as good a reason as any for tying a particular pattern. They also work, which is the other reason.

Jay paddled to the deep water, while I worked out along the weed beds. Neither spot was any better than the other, he said. It soon became obvious that damsel nymphs were boiling up out of every inch of bottom, and the trout were everywhere, feeding actively, but languidly, as if, sure, this is great, but we're sort of used to it, you know?

Jay and I were both into fish within a few minutes, and it was hot. The strikes were nearly always the same: a dull thud in the rod as the fly just stopped in the water, then an almost audible thrumming in the line as it went tight, and vibrated from the wrist out. Then, after what seemed like a second or two of indecision on the part of the fish, the no-nonsense run began, during which you had better not have line tangled around your flippers.

Some fish bored deeply, others jumped. A few were so big and portly they tried to jump, but couldn't, and ended up wallowing almost pitifully on the surface.

We must have taken a dozen trout each that morning, all rainbows. None were under eighteen inches, none that we landed were over twenty-two. I took some color photographs. The fish we managed to break off may have been bigger yet (as you automatically assume) or the results of operator error, or maybe strained and weakened tippet knots. Let's say they were bigger. Let's say that especially because Jay had caught, earlier that year from the same pond, a seven-pound brook trout, one of only a handful of brookies that had survived a planting some years ago.

Seven pounds is a hell of a big trout, let alone a brook trout. As firm and healthy as those rainbows were, the biggest ones we caught that morning still only weighed five, tops.

Did I say "only"? You know what I mean.

It had been furious at first, and had then petered off in roughly fifteen-minute increments until the strikes were noticeably few and far between, our arms were sore from fighting fish, and you'd have to look for quite a while to find a damsel in the water. At about ten o'clock Jay switched from a damsel to his secret leech pattern, and began trolling the deep trough.

I took a shore break. A belly boat is probably the most comfortable thing to fish from, with the possible exception of a lawn chair, but it's still good to get out after a few hours, especially when you forgot to pee before you got in that morning.

And so we fell into the program. The damsels in the early mornings were like clockwork, always there, and always good. From ten o'clock to about noon you could pound up a few more trout on leech patterns. Then, in the late afternoon, *something* would happen. It was never quite the same twice, but the fish would feed, and after a while you could figure it out.

Of course, if so much as a single big caddis showed itself, there was no guessing. That was the one bug that every piece of trout water seems to have: the one the fish will eat, whatever else they may or may not be doing. It was the mythical sure thing, and we had it covered. We'd captured a few naturals the first night and I had copied them at the portable fly-tying kit using light wire hooks and lots and lots of ginger hackle to stand them up on the water.

In fact, we had it *all* covered for once—hatches, flies, timing, place—and the fish were all big. It does sometimes happen that way.

———

The hot afternoons were down time. There were naps—some planned, some inadvertent—and I made entries in the notebook

that seemed at the time to have something to do with the story
I was supposed to be working on. It wasn't the story itself, nor
quite an outiine, nor all of it even on the subject at hand, for
that matter. During the all-nighter I'd pull back home to get
the thing out on time I would discard page after page of it,
wondering vaguely what the hell I'd meant by this or that. This
mess is what a writer is usually talking about when he refers to
his precious "notes."

These were long, slow, hypnotic breaks with the craziness of
some very fast fishing just over with, and more of it coming up
in the evening, as soon as the sunlight slanted and the air began
to cool off again. I'd lounge on a flat spot between the truck and
the pond, using the beached float tube as an easy chair,
notebook on knee, pen in one hand, can of lukewarm beer in the
other. If pressed, I could say I was working, but I'd catch myself
thinking, for instance, that it was going to be good to see Susan
when I got back. Not aching to go home or anything, just
thinking how it would definitely be okay when I *did* get back. I
mean, you do have to go home sometime, right?

Regardless of what you've heard, it's entirely permissible to
miss the girlfriend while on a fishing trip, especially between
hatches, but you do have to watch it when you have a pen in
your hand. If you're not careful, all your sunsets will be
orgasmic, and all your trout will be pulsing and throbbing.

———

One afternoon we drove into town for a good meal. Not that
we were exactly starving, but we'd been putting away conven-
ience store camp food that does little more than keep you going.
Jay had set the tone the first night with a frozen pizza cooked in
the propane oven. It was okay, although gnawing it off the
charred cardboard was a chore.

Town was Encampment, Wyoming, on the small river of the
same name. Downtown consisted of a general store, the Bear
Trap Cafe, the Mangy Moose Tavern, and very little else. Over
prime rib at the Bear Trap I asked Jay about the Encampment,

and it turned out to be yet another in a growing list of little streams a guy really ought to get around to fishing sometime. There are so many little streams, so many cafés. Some days it's almost too much to contemplate.

"I've heard there are trout in it," he said; "I guess it can be pretty good."

The waitress came over to ask how the food was. "Great," we said, which was not an overstatement.

"I'll tell him you said he was a pretty good cook for poor white trash," she said, nodding toward the kitchen door. I smiled, thinking she was surely kidding.

"Leroy!" she yelled. "These guys say you're a good cook for white trash."

I stopped chewing. Jay glanced around to check the location of all the exits.

Leroy, all 250 pounds of him, came to the kitchen door, gave us a blank stare, and winked at the woman.

Local humor.

———

That was the evening the net disappeared. I had an especially big rainbow right in front of the tube—twenty-two inches easy, maybe twenty-four, a glorious, side-of-bacon-sized trout—and when I reached smoothly for the net where it should have been fastened to the D ring on my right, it just wasn't there.

I'd never landed a trout that big by hand before. It wasn't easy.

This was a wooden net and should have just been floating out there somewhere, but it was gone. I looked for a long time while Jay caught fish, occasionally saying things over his shoulder like, "Maybe it's still in the truck," to which I'd answer, "No, I just had the damned thing ten minutes ago."

The night was warm and still, stars were out, coyotes were yipping close by. My net was lost in Wyoming.

That was the one night when the trout got a little spooky and leader shy for some reason. This naturally calls for lighter tippets

and smaller flies—the standard trout technician countermove.
Fine, but these were very large trout, and as I rerigged with a
smaller fly and thinner monofilament, I realized that this would
make the fish easier to hook, but also harder to land, so that the
closer I got to success, the closer I also got to failure.

An interesting thought. Also an apparent dead end.

———

As I mentioned, the trailer didn't have electricity, but Jay is a
bit of a gadget freak and had a tiny, battery-operated television
set in there. We turned it on that night to catch the news.

The picture was grainy and the sound was poor, but we could
make out that a large building somewhere had fallen on a whole
bunch of people, killing most of them. It occurred to me that,
out here, things the size of a K-Mart could fall out of the sky all
week, and probably not kill anything but a few prairie dogs.

So there was more trouble out in the world, which we could
have guessed, but probably could have lived without hearing
about. Frankly, it was hard to feel too sorry about it. This stuff
happens all the time, and it's become a survival skill to avoid
letting your heart break every single time.

The guy doing the southern Wyoming weather report didn't
seem too sorry either. He came on right after the film of this
horrible accident and said that weather prediction up there is
easy. "It'll either be too hot, too cold, or too windy tomorrow,
ha, ha."

———

Back in Encampment, Jay had made a phone call, and so had
I. It became obvious that we were leaving the next day, but not
before fishing those damsel flies one more time. In the past few
days I had landed more twenty-inch and bigger trout than in the
two or three previous seasons combined. Still, a few more
wouldn't hurt.

I didn't waste any valuable time looking for the net again. I'd be pissed off enough about that later to snap at the guy at the fly shop, but at the moment the trout would be biting. I had two of the damsel nymphs left, and, if those got lost, a couple of small olive leeches that should work. I knew what should work now.

It was the kind of morning I'd come to expect. I even learned how to hand-land the big, slimy fish with a little bit of style; came out of the damsel hatch with one fly left; switched confidently to the leech and kept catching fish. Put simply, I was happy.

We'd agreed to leave around noon, at the beginning of the long dead stretch that would last until evening. It wasn't that long a trip home from here. We'd be back about the time the rise began. I knew how it all worked now, and that's as good a time as any to go.

CHAPTER 16

BRITISH COLUMBIA

Overheard in British Columbia:

Fisherman: "How long have you guys been saying 'eh?' at the end of every sentence?"

Bush Pilot: "About as long as you Americans have been saying, 'Huh?'"

———

Bush pilots, those guys who fly float planes around in remote areas—usually in Canada or Alaska—are the victims of a stereotype. We picture them dressed in greasy leather jackets, goggles, and silk scarves as they climb into their sputtering antique airplanes after banging around inside the engine for twenty minutes with a wrench, and then taking a good, long pull on a hip flask.

The guy's name is something like Crazy Bill, and as you buckle your seat belt he says cheerfully, "Don't worry, I haven't lost a passenger in weeks." For now you've forgotten about the lake you're going to fish. All you want to do at the moment is live through this.

That's the romantic notion of bush pilots that's still fostered by sportsmen, and especially writers, to make their trip into the interior of someplace or other sound like even more of an adventure than it really was. Like all romantic notions, it was probably once true, and it's still what we want to believe. It's probably fair to say that most of the pilots still have a touch of it in them, but *just* a touch, and only because the clients seem to like it.

When we're safe back at home we want our bush pilot to have been a maniacal barnstormer, so it sounds as if we not only caught fish, but also looked death in the face in order to do it. On-site, though, things are a little different. There you're looking for Captain Doug of the Canadian Float Plane Air Force: a solid, clearheaded, clean-cut family man who holds traditional values and flies by the book; a guy who is young enough to be sharp as hell, but old enough to have stopped counting at four or five thousand hours in the air.

VFR (visual flight rules) only. No local color and no barrel rolls.

———

Jay Allman and I were fishing out of a lodge in the interior plateau of British Columbia, about 250 air miles (or 700 road miles) north of Vancouver. The place was about as posh as I can stand. We had a tight one-room cabin with a good wood stove to ourselves, and ate two meals a day in the simple dining room at the main lodge in answer to a dinner bell. Everything was simple and matter-of-factly competent, including the meals, which is all I want from this kind of operation. You can pay two or three times more, but in the end all you really get is fancier food and more expensive booze. The fishing will be about the same, and it seems odd to eat and drink better on a fishing trip than you would at home.

In the morning after breakfast we'd stroll down to the dock, board a float plane, and be flown wherever we wanted to go to fish. There was no night flying, so we'd be back for supper. This was prewar-style, high-tech fishing.

Between the three airplanes it took to get from Denver to the dirt airstrip at Anahim Lake—the last leg on Wilderness Airlines—plus flying out every day to fish one or sometimes two lakes, I was in the air a lot for a guy who doesn't care to fly all that much.

This isn't exactly a phobia, it's just that I have some misgivings and suspicions about aircraft. I believe, for instance, that fear somehow helps keep the plane up in the air, so someone on board should be at least a little scared at all times as a basic safety precaution. In a small plane with no more than three passengers, I like to cover that base myself, just in case everyone else gets distracted by a moose or something.

Most days we flew with Doug in a big, powerful, forty-some-year-old de Havilland Beaver. I don't know a lot about these things, but I do know the Beaver is one of the classic bush planes of all time: large, droning, reliable, and familiar. It has never been improved upon.

By the time we'd lugged our gear down to the dock in the morning, the Beaver, and the newer, flashier Cessna, were already warming up. Some days there was time for a second or even third cup of coffee as we waited for the thick, chilly fog to clear. This was mid-September, very close to winter that far north. The prop wash would make a current in the still air, blowing cold mist into our faces as we stood carefully on the icy dock.

It felt good, and I was happy to be there. For years I'd said that mornings like this elsewhere reminded me of British Columbia, even though I'd never been there. Now I'd be able to say that with authority.

To some, flying into roadless backcountry in a plane that's older than the pilot or any of the passengers would be a little freaky, but that's actually the part I found to be most comforting. I figure anything that's been in the air long enough to have become a classic has built up some excellent karma. Another more practical advantage is that virtually all of a Beaver's controls are either mechanical or hydraulic, to keep surprise electrical failures to a minimum. This one had a fairly new engine, too.

You fly low in a float plane—by airline standards—taking twisting routes to this or that lake, flying between mountains as if you were on a dirt road. The fact that there *are* no roads makes the plane the equivalent of a pickup truck. That's comforting, too.

The ride is sometimes rough, the cabin drafty and loud. There's little conversation. Now and then someone will grab your shoulder, point, and shout, "Caribou!" You nod and holler back, "Right!"

It was fun. After only a day or two of it, I had to strain in order to stay worried.

———

The lodge itself sits on the shore of a large, banana-shaped lake in flat, wet, wooded country full of resident moose and grizzly bears that migrate through on their way to the coast for the salmon runs. A few miles to the West are the Coast Mountains, and farther west yet is the Pacific Ocean. There are lakes and creeks everywhere, either "hundreds" of each or "countless numbers of them," depending on who you ask.

The lodge was built in the 1950s by the present owner's father, who came up to British Columbia after the Second World War and started guiding hunters and fishermen at the end of what was then a seven-hundred-mile, vehicle-eating road from Vancouver. There's still only the one main road, but now it swings west through Tweedsmuir Park and goes all the way over to Bella Coola on the ocean side.

The lodge building is made of logs. It's small and low-ceilinged, designed to hold the heat from the stone fireplace. There are some modern firearms hanging on the wall, and also Dad's old .38-55 Winchester with a dinged-up stock and most of the bluing rubbed off. Over the mantle, just below the mount of the big rainbow trout, is his Jim Payne bamboo fly rod with one broken tip to show that it was used.

This doesn't quite constitute a shrine. Dad is retired, and lives in a cabin just down the shore a little ways. I'd like to have met him, but I never did. He had arranged to be off limits.

The main fish in this area is the rainbow trout; the salmon and steelhead are on the other side of the mountains, running up the rivers from the ocean. That's where the groovy fly-fishermen go to catch the big, silver, sea run fish. The interior is considered to be more plebian.

They say it's the Kamloops rainbow east of the mountains, although apparently there is some doubt among scientists as to the fish's exact classification. Whatever, it's a sturdy-looking trout: your standard wild rainbow, just a little longer in the body and deeper in the gut than most, and fat.

In midsummer there are hatches of insects and the fish will eat dry flies. By September it's streamers: a small, local version of the Muddler Minnow, and the Wooly Bugger, which they call a Wooly *Booger*.

A five-pound rainbow here is exceptional. That's the size of the one over the fireplace. Three pounds is good.

There are also a couple of lakes in the mountains that have landlocked coastal cutthroats, and there's a local story about that. It seems there was this old trapper who found some lakes with no fish in them. That bothered him, so he hauled in a pair of cutts on a pack mule from the river lower down—a male and a female. Some years later, voilá, the lake full of cutthroats.

I tell this *as* a local story, not as if it was necessarily true. But the fish are there.

And then there are the Dolly Vardens. Word was they were in two large, connected lakes, they were larger than most, and they could be taken on flies. It sounded obscure and exotic, and we wanted to see it. Jay wanted a big Dolly to mount. I had never caught a big one and wanted to.

For that matter, I may never have caught a *real* one. I'd caught some bull trout in Montana, which some say is just a Dolly and some say isn't. As with the difference of opinion over the Kamloops rainbows, when the scientists disagree, I don't know exactly what to do about it. Go fishing, I guess.

It was a wild ride to Knot Lakes. We flew straight west toward the mountains, and it seemed as if we just gained enough altitude before we got there to be able to bank between some of the lower peaks heading for snowcaps and glaciers looming up ahead through the clear disk of the propeller. There's something thrilling about looking up at rock cliffs from an airplane. A few miles east of Pandemonium Pass, we turned south down the narrow slot of the Atnarko River and followed that upstream to the headwater lakes.

There are two of them strung together, both are miles long, skinny and dizzyingly far down there when you first fly over the lip of the canyon. The lakes are narrow and they're an opaque milky green color from the surrounding glaciers. It doesn't even look like water until you're low enough to see the liquid texture of it.

The place for Dollys, the pilot said, was where a glacial stream fed into the lake. Jay and I didn't like the dirty look of the water at first, either from the air or the ground. The lake itself was that glacial-melt tint, and the fan of the current from the little stream was gray. You couldn't see more than a foot into it. But, although the pilots aren't exactly guides and don't claim to be, you at least start where they tell you to. They're bound to know more about it than you do.

It worked. The fish seemed to be cruising at the edges of the current as it fanned into the lake. The stream forked just upcurrent, so there were actually two small inlets about fifty yards apart with a quarter acre of backwater between them.

We'd been told the preferred lure was a long, thin silver spoon with a prismatic finish on one side fished in fifteen or twenty feet of water. With that as a hint, we'd tied some weighted white-and-silver bucktail streamers, and I had a few six-inch-long bass flies, just in case.

Fifteen or twenty feet is really too deep for fly-fishing, but you know how you have these points you have to prove. We worked at it for a while, using sink-tip lines and, finally, split shot on the noses of the flies to sink them faster.

We satisfied ourselves that it could be done by landing a few fish, at which point Jay reeled in and switched to a spinning rig.

Having more to prove, I guess, I stayed with the fly rod. At least for a while.

Dollys aren't considered to be an especially classy game fish, probably because they're deepwater fish-eaters that are not known to rise to dry flies. Along with lake trout, grayling, and a few others, they're in that class of fish that are generally considered to be one step down on the scale from rainbows, browns, brookies, and cutts.

Dollys are a breed of char. These were a grayish olive overall (not unlike the color of the water they were in) and to my eye they looked a lot like Mackinaws, only with faint orange, troutlike spots on their sides. I've seen pictures of them where the fins go orange with white borders and the bellies have a pink cast, making them look like a brook trout that's not quite right. The ones I caught did not look like that, nor quite like Montana bull trout either.

Jay had switched to the spinning rod and was easily lobbing his spoon clear out to where the current settled in the lake and the water changed color. Then he'd let the lure sink for a count of five or so before beginning the retrieve.

To get that kind of distance, I had to cast my sink-tip line and heavy streamer as far out into the current as I could, and then feed line until the flow of the inlet sucked my fly out far enough. Then I'd mend the line into the quieter water, let it sink for five minutes, and finally begin to strip it back.

Jay was fishing out ten casts to my one, but I was, by god, *fly-fishing*—or at least fishing with a fly rod.

I was standing there waiting for my sink-tip to get down the required twenty feet, amusing myself by trying to exactly formulate the point I was trying to make, when Jay hooked a heavy fish. As soon as I heard him say, "Oh, shit," I started reeling in my line to avoid a tangle. This is the common etiquette when someone anywhere near you gets a fish on that will take some playing to land. It also gives you the opportunity to sit back and watch the performance, and maybe even to make some obvious suggestions. You always think you could do it better.

The fight of a big Dolly isn't that entertaining unless you happen to be the one holding the rod. There were no jumps or tail walks, and the runs weren't what you'd call blistering. The fish would grind out line, Jay would gain it back, and little by little the two of them came closer together. This went on long enough that I started getting anxious to fish again. The pilot put down his magazine, climbed out of the cockpit, and came over to watch about the time Jay was reaching for his landing net.

This was a fine fish: healthy, deep-bellied, a good twenty-four inches long, plenty big enough to hang on the wall as a respectable specimen. I dug out the camera and took the required hero shot. Then Jay whopped the fish on the head, laid it in a few inches of still water to keep it fresh, and piled rocks on top of it to keep it from drifting away.

The fishing never was hot and heavy in any one spot, so we assumed the Dollys were prowling around rather than holding. In theory you can do fine in this situation by just casting over and over to the same water on the premise that sooner or later a fish will swim by. In practice, you want to move around, if only to have something to do between strikes. And, after all, we'd gone to some trouble to get ourselves into British Columbia. I think we both wanted to scout around a little.

We tried up and down the bank. We even got into the belly boats and trolled around the plume of the inlet. As long as we stayed in the neighborhood of the dirty current we got strikes and landed some fish, though none of them were terribly large. Somewhere in there I got out my own spinning rod in the interest of efficiency.

I'll say one thing in favor of waiting for your sinking fly line to slowly work its way to the desired depth: it gives you time to look at the scenery. We were on a long, green lake in a deep, forested gorge with the Concubine Peaks to the west, capped on the southern end by Monarch Mountain—3,533 meters high. Back home in Colorado that would be 11,591 feet. A damned nice snow-covered mountain cuddling a couple of glaciers on its lower slopes.

When it was time to pack up and fly out, Jay went to collect his fish. It was gone.

"What!?" I said. "You mean *gone*!?"

Jay pointed sadly to where the rocks he'd piled on his big Dolly Varden had been rudely tossed aside.

This was rough, geologically new glacier country. What passed for a beach was a strip of fist-sized cobbles that even a large animal wouldn't leave tracks in. There was no blood, no guts, no fish head in evidence, so the trophy had been stolen whole rather than eaten on the spot. If there was ever a wet drag mark it would have had plenty of time to dry.

"Prob'ly an otter," the pilot said. "Lots of otters around here."

Jay was not pleased. He glared into the tangle of willows the little glacial stream came out of. His big fish was in there somewhere, most likely in the belly of a happy mammal who could now take the day off. Jay took it like a man, there not being much of an alternative.

On the flight out, shouting over the engine, I told Jay it was just as likely to have been a grizzly as an otter. The bears were known to be there, people came to hunt them, and there was that snarling mount back at the lodge. With no sand for tracks, who could say for sure? Anyway, it would make a better story. So by the time we sat down for supper at the lodge, that's how it was: an enormous fish cleverly caught, heroically landed, and stolen by a slavering, possibly rabid, griz.

Hell, we were lucky to be alive to tell about it.

There was a new party in that night, four guys from Vancouver who'd come to do some serious drinking and a little fishing, in that order. They liked the story. They liked it so much that they claimed it as their own. By the time they'd finished with it, it was Elvis who'd stolen the fish, while his faithful attack-trained grizzly bear kept watch. Then they'd both hightailed it into the bushes where they'd boarded an ominously humming UFO to conduct tests. We could only guess at what dastardly purpose they had in mind.

I was toying with the idea of calling the *National Enquirer* when the leader of this bunch, the biggest, loudest guy, handed me the largest bottle of Kahlua I'd ever seen, saying, "Have some, it's medicinal. Cures everything but the dropsy—which of course it causes."

———

For most of the trip we fished for the rainbows, got casual about riding in the planes, and saw what seemed like endless, empty country. One day we flew into a small mountain lake and saw another float plane parked on it. Another party of fishermen, or maybe moose hunters.

"I'll take you somewhere else," the pilot said, "No use coming all this way to fish in a crowd."

The single most revealing thing about any part of the world is what constitutes a crowd.

The landscape was all eerily familiar. The lakes were generally larger than the ones back home, but the mountains were the same shape and operated on the same scheme, even to the lodgepole pine and aspen forests, and the mountain chickadees and steller's jays flitting around in them.

The differences were very real, though. I'd just get to feeling at home when I'd see what looked like elk on a hillside, but then they'd turn out to be caribou. I'd seen shed caribou antlers in the wild before, but never the animals themselves. There were Players navy cut cigarettes and Kokanee beer—union-made right there in British Columbia—and there were the loons, those big, fish-eating birds that always seem to be floating too low in the water. They'd patrol the lakes by day and then laugh like maniacs at night. It's the wildest sound you'll ever hear. I tried to remember the story of why the loon giggles, but it had been a long time since I'd heard it back in Minnesota. All I could recall was that it sounded like the kind of sappy Indian legend a white person would make up, full of unrequited love and suicide.

There's always this tendency I have to imagine spending a winter in a strange part of the world. In the north country, winter tells the real story. You can't say you really know what a place is like if all you ever did there was swat mosquitoes and slather on sunscreen.

One night I asked the owner how the winters were and he said, "I hear they're rough. We spend winters going to sportsmen's shows in the States."

I get this from my father, who was something of a sporting historian. "Imagine this in 1840," he'd say. "The best you'd have then would be a wooden canoe and a percussion lock rifle." Dad liked to hunt and fish, but he had the kind of intellectual take on wilderness that is not uncommon. He knew full well that he was never going to vanish into it with a pack on his back never to be seen or heard from again, but he wanted it to be out there so someone else could do that.

And maybe also just in case he changed his mind one day. Which, of course, he never did.

It was also from Dad that I caught this thing for Canada. The only parts of it I've seen at close hand (not counting airports) have been wild and even largely trackless—the kind of country anyone would love—but I also like the people. That's something that hits me right away. In the airport in Seattle people don't even want to look at you, but when you get off the plane in Vancouver half an hour later someone walks right up to you and says, "Goin' fishing, eh?"

Ask why there are still portraits of the queen all over the place after all these years of independence from England and someone will say, "I guess no one took 'em down yet."

During a lunch break one day on a lake surrounded by tundra and a few struggling fir trees, Doug the bush pilot put the difference between Canada and the United States clearly. "You guys want everyone to be the same, and you have this religious thing about your government; this total devotion you expect. We encourage diversity and see our government as a business arrangement, I mean, someone's gotta run things, that's all."

And there's plenty of room, too, which makes a great subliminal difference. Someone once pointed out that the Canadian consciousness is that of a people with real wilderness at their backs.

Sure, it's changing. This area has really only been fished for the forty years since World War II, but it's opened up now by Wilderness Airlines and squadrons of bush pilots so that already you can talk to fishermen who honestly remember when the trout were bigger and there were more of them.

Sometimes I think if I hear that one more time I'll take a swing at the guy who said it.

The people at the lodge said they were hoping to gradually phase from spin fishermen into fly-fishermen in the future because they felt the understandable need to promote catch-and-release fishing, and the latter group is more likely to buy into that. And also because fly-fishing has the reputation for being a big money sport, although I'll testify that it doesn't have to be. Basically, they want sports who will take home a few smoked rainbows and maybe one big one for the wall instead of the trunks full of dead fish that go out now.

They're working on the change, but their answer to most inquiries about how to fish is still "troll deep," and they have yet to dismantle the industrial-sized fish smoker. Lest I sound too righteous there, let me say that I brought back a tastefully small package of absolutely scrumptious smoked wild Kamloops rainbows that I mostly hoarded, carefully doling out samples to close friends.

They're also talking about making the lodge bigger so they can bring in more sports and feed more people at a time. That may be necessary in terms of profit margin, but it would be too bad otherwise. It's a sweet old building—about the size of an average one-story house—where you can feel blissfully safe on a cold fall night.

———

Jay, it seemed, had this score to settle, so before it was all over Doug dropped us off for one more day at Knot Lakes, and then flew off to run some unspecified errand, promising to be back before dark.

One way to feel fabulously alone and on your own is to stand there in the middle of nowhere in British Columbia listening to the bass drone of a de Havilland Beaver fading into nothingness. You've got a fly rod, a tuna fish sandwich, a couple of beers, and no sleeping bag.

Low and behold, Jay caught another big Dolly from almost the exact spot where he took the first one, and this one was even bigger. It taped out to exactly 30 and ¼ inches. Jay all but sat on it until the plane came back for us.

Of course, by this time I'd come to believe our story about the bear myself. I wasn't what you'd call freaked, but I did keep thinking I heard twigs snapping behind me. Being afoot and unarmed in grizzly country is a little like having had too much coffee: you don't think about it every minute, but there's still a sort of constant buzz. But then, I guess we do all this for the buzz, so I shouldn't complain.

———

I'm sitting at home now looking at a map of Tweedsmuir Park and some of the surrounding country—roughly fifteen thousand square kilometers with one road through it and two small settlements—trying to get some kind of purchase on the aforementioned buzz. To tell you the truth, the fishing was okay, perfectly acceptable, although I've had better in terms of numbers and size, and closer to home, too.

What sticks in my mind is this: one day, flying in the newer, faster, smaller Cessna with Duncan, the owner, we stopped briefly at a lake where there was an outpost cabin. The errand was to pick up a bicycle pump so we could inflate our belly boats when we finally got to where we were supposed to be going in the first place. Two fishermen, one pilot, and a pair of fully inflated float tubes will not fit in a Cessna.

The weather had looked grim on the way in with a big front moving in from the Pacific, and by the time we had the pump and were ready to take off again, a good snowstorm had closed in over us. So we sat out on the lake in the plane, bobbing around like a big silver duck, waiting for the sky to clear a little.

After half an hour the snow petered out a bit, and a small hole leading to blue sky appeared.

"How about that?" I asked the pilot.

"If we fly through that," he said, "we could be up there all day, running out of fuel, looking for another hole to fly back down through. And god only knows where we'd end up."

"Oh," I said.

The hole closed, the conversation drifted into silence and stayed that way for a while. Snow was collecting on the wings. Finally the pilot said, "Looks like we'll be spending the winter here, eh?"

On the trip back to Denver, Wilderness Airlines was late getting into Vancouver because of the same storm ("What else is new," said the guy at the United ticket counter), and Jay and I embarked on a more civilized adventure involving missed flights and lost luggage. I remember drinking overpriced beer in the airport bar in Seattle while Jay's big Dolly Varden sat in a box on the floor slowly thawing. They'd had to tape an extra four inches of cardboard onto the end of the box to accommodate the fish's tail.

I don't remember the name of that lake now—maybe I never even knew it at the time—but I remember how it looked as we sat out there waiting for the clouds to lift and the snow to stop so we could get on with it and catch some fish. It was the moment every good trip has when, by design or force of circumstances, you stop moving, fishing, and thinking and just look at where the hell you are.

In this case, where you are is in the middle of a trout lake in British Columbia with winter settling in. You have a fast plane, a hot pilot, a tank of gas, and nowhere to go.

CHAPTER 17

THE
TROUT WARS

Sometimes, because of the logic of the poetry, the name of a place is hauntingly accurate. For instance, Phantom Canyon is called that because if you weren't taken out and shown, you wouldn't know it was there. Lots of people don't.

It's a deep, sudden crease through some otherwise ordinary dry, high plains rangeland just south of the Wyoming border. There's a trout stream at the bottom of it, the North Fork of the Cache la Poudre River. More than one person has commented, "Hell, I didn't even know the Poudre *had* a north fork."

The surrounding country is nice enough, complete with cactus and antelope, but a bit shy on water holes: the kind of place where you can feel a little silly with fly rods and waders in the car.

Steve Peterson was driving, and during a lull in the conversation A.K. gave me one of those puzzled but still amused looks that say, "Not that I mind all that much, but where the hell is this guy taking us?"

We've both had that kind of mixed feeling before on the way to a secret spot. It's a tempered suspicion. If the place wasn't queer or camouflaged in some way, it probably wouldn't be a secret. In a sense, the more unlikely the countryside looks the more promising it is.

This often calls for a little faith.

The two-rut dirt road passes through one locked gate and an electric fence, then just ends at the rim of the canyon. You *do* see it coming, but only from far enough away that you wouldn't drive right into it. It's just there: a phantom canyon.

Way down in there you see trees—ponderosa pine, juniper, and cottonwood, mostly—with a border of brush along a narrow stream. From up on the lip in the month of October, it's green, orange, yellow, brown, and silvery blue. It's also very far away.

If the trail hadn't been there, the first order of business would have been to carefully scout a way in, figuring a well-worn game trail would be the best shot. It would have taken some doing to locate a route that wouldn't leave you dead-ended halfway down, with the kind of ruined visual perspective that would make you lost, even though you knew exactly where you were. This is the kind of canyon you don't just start into without planning.

As it was, getting in was easy, on what seemed like miles of nearly geometric switchbacks. We could see that getting back out that night was going to be a real slow-paced, one-step-at-a-time grunt—not something you'd have to worry about all day, although you might start dreading it when the sunlight crawled out of the canyon and started up that tall east wall.

I've always loved these little canyon streams. Whatever the surrounding countryside is like—lush, semiarid, forest, plains—the canyon drops away like a trapdoor into a secret room. It's shady down in there, and cooler. In the winter it's *colder*. The farther into it you go, the more palpable the space above you becomes. The narrower the sky gets the more it resembles a roof, and suddenly it doesn't quite feel like you're outside anymore.

The days are shorter in a canyon, but the abundant moisture from the stream still grows thicker, higher trees and more underbrush than the surrounding landscape. The tallest, straightest ponderosa pines I've ever seen have all been in canyons, out of the wind, and with plenty of water.

Down on the floor of it, things seem to be in miniature. Six pines standing more or less together seem like a grove, if not a wood; a quarter acre of uninterrupted grass passes for a meadow. The stream itself isn't very big either, but even in the fall when the water is low, it fills the place up. It is, after all, flowing down the very notch it has cut for itself, so the stream fits the canyon like your foot would fit a custom-made hiking boot.

Every canyon seems remote, and you can add inaccessibility points for depth and steepness. As long as we're keeping score, let's also add points for all the people who don't know about this particular one, for the fourteen-thousand-acre private ranch that insulates it, and that, this October, it took connections as well as a good hike to get in.

And then there was the name itself. This was *Phantom Canyon.* I still can't say that without trying to sound like Vincent Price.

Needless to say, I was properly jazzed by the time I reached the stream. A.K. looked like he was doing some kind of primitive dance step until I realized he was trying to put his waders on before he'd stopped walking. Even Steve, who'd been in and out of there dozens of times by then, was looking around with a silly, self-congratulatory grin on his face. There's no place on earth like the bottom of a canyon.

———

The stream itself looked new, in that raw way canyon streams have. There's a sense that the place is still being carved, that it isn't finished and never will be. The boulders that are littered around still have crisp edges free of lichens from where they broke out of the walls and fell in. If you look up on the slopes you see eons of exposed geology, but then some of this looks like it happened yesterday.

Days later, with nothing better to do, I would try to get hold of the idea that the canyon was getting imperceptibly deeper right under my feet as I stood in the stream, but at the moment there were these rising trout, and when I started looking at the water to see what kind of bug they were eating, Steve said, "Don't worry about that, just fish a number sixteen Adams."

The trout were homegrown rainbows and browns that may have been stocked here in years past or, more likely, had noodled their way up from the main river to make themselves at home. Those are the two best guesses, but no one really knows for sure. The fish are just there, like the canyon itself. They're not natives (they'd have to be cutthroats for that) but they're unquestionably wild, born-in-the-stream fish that have been left alone for a long time.

I got several strikes within my first dozen casts, but missed them all because I was setting the hook too quickly. These trout were completely fooled by the fly; they'd take it casually, with none of the suspicions or second thoughts that smarter fish seem to exhibit. I was trying too hard.

Let's not say "smarter fish," let's say "trout that have been pestered a lot by humans."

When I slowed down, pacing myself to the trout, I started to connect. The first one I hooked was a rainbow that was rising in a narrow braid of current behind and to one side of a small rock—an excellent holding spot where the flow funneled the insects from a yard-wide strip of current down to a couple of inches. The cast was a good eighteen inches short, and I was about to pick it up and try again when the fish swam over slowly, looked at the fly for a second, and then ate it. Just like that.

It was almost too easy.

There were six miles of stream for us to fish that day—more than three fishermen could cover without hurrying. Leapfrogging upstream, we may have worked half of it, or maybe just a third, I don't really know. When things are in small scale, you slow to a more organic pace and stop worrying about what you haven't seen yet. When nothing is very far away, you feel free to go take a look at a strange rock or a pretty bush. You end up going along a small canyon stream the way a dog goes up an alley: busy, but vacillating between purpose and distraction, and with no destination in mind.

The stream was in its fall flow, so in the riffles and shallower runs, the water was about as low as it could get and still be fishable. There were a few spooky, but eager trout in the faster water, but most were at the heads and tails of the deep pools. These were the wintering-over holes, and there were lots of them. Some seemed almost bottomless even in the low flow. From twenty or thirty feet up on the canyon wall, you could look into the clear water and see only a ring of rocks around a deep slot that went from cold blue to shapeless black.

A small stream can be rough on its trout population, especially when the winter flows go way down through parts of the year, but these deep holes make the difference. This is why most small streams—however good they are—aren't actually packed with fish. There will only be as many trout in them as can crowd comfortably into the deepest water through the cold months.

The trout fed methodically, and with a noticeably unconcerned air about them. They would eat an Adams dry fly—an 18 to a 14, though the size 16 worked best—and the larger ones would jump on a #6 olive or black Weedless Wooly Bugger. They would spook at the sight of a looming human form or the shadow of a fly line because those things would remind them of a stooping osprey, but leaders didn't seem to bother them, and flies were food, even when the drift was less than perfect. Never mind that I never saw anything on the water as large as a #16 fly all day.

This was innocence, something I hadn't encountered in recent seasons because I'd been fishing too much where too many others fished. These trout weren't huge or fat—they were streamlined in the finest sense of the word—but they were robust and hard. Simply put, they had done well for themselves. And they weren't stupid or idiotically easy to catch, just unaccustomed to humans and their tricks.

It all reminded me of something, and I realized what as A.K. and I sat on a little four-by-six-foot patch of green grass eating sandwiches and pulling on canteens. The last time I'd seen fish act like this was in British Columbia, and before that the

Northwest Territories, places where fishing pressure was not the rule, but the exception.

It was one of those momentary revelations: it's not so much that this is easy, it's just the way it's supposed to be. This is why all those old guys are still running around saying, "If you know how to fish, all you need is a Renegade and a Rio Grande King." Before catch-and-release fly-fishing—before the need for it—it was all like this.

As wild trout will, the fish came in all sizes. Mostly they were between about nine and sixteen inches. A few were smaller: little guys who fed in the poorer spots because they weren't big enough yet to compete for the better ones. And, naturally, a few were also larger. A.K. turned one that might have gone eighteen or twenty, I popped a streamer off in one that was also pretty hefty.

On the drive in Steve had told of a hog (I seem to remember five or six pounds being mentioned). He'd caught it several times, and now it would no longer take the Adams. It was getting difficult, it wanted a slimmer, more modern pattern.

You could say this trout had been educated, or possibly that he'd been corrupted, made cynical. Then again, you could say he was now enlightened. Whatever, he was very big and he was getting hard to catch. Steve showed us around graciously and unselfishly, even to the point where it cut into his own fishing. He did not show us where the hog lived. We didn't ask, figuring that was fair enough.

———

Okay, it's time I told you that Phantom Canyon is a preserve owned by the Nature Conservancy. At the time we fished it, it was scheduled to be opened to the public the following summer at the rate of six rods per day, three days a week. Steve took us in the previous fall for a preview. The place had been fished some then, but it was still very close to being virgin.

Steve is a trips program coordinator for the western branch of the conservancy. I know what a trips program coordinator is—he's sort of a combination big-ticket fund-raiser and fishing guide—but before the Phantom Canyon trip A.K. and I had only the usual vague information on the Nature Conservancy: we understood that it was some sort of conservation group, but essentially we'd only heard the name mentioned here and there.

It turns out there's a reason for that. Steve said the organization is consciously low-profile.

This all started back in 1951 when an obscure group of scientists known as the Ecologist's Union renamed themselves the Nature Conservancy and started buying land. Their charter was simple and straightforward: these guys were interested in species diversity, or, more properly, the growing lack thereof in the environment, and they had decided to try and do something about it. Since then they have preserved nearly three million acres in the United States, and have become what *National Geographic* magazine recently called, "One of the youngest, least known, and most successful environmental groups in this country."

What they do usually works something like this: a chunk of privately owned real estate is identified as habitat for one or more threatened or endangered species, be they plant or animal. Places like that are not hard to find. The list of species that are in some kind of trouble is a long one.

The conservancy then acquires the land and turns it into a "preserve."

How a piece of land is managed depends on the particular situation. If the habitat is so delicate that any human activity would threaten it, then there is no human activity, except for the odd scientist who presumably knows where not to step.

If some recreational access (fishing, hunting, bird-watching, nature walking, etc.) would be okay, then it's allowed, usually on a limited basis with no fee.

The conservancy decides, and it doesn't have to get approval from you or me or the state or federal government. This is private land. It can do what it likes with it.

The idea is to identify these critical habitats and then take them out of the loop of land speculation and development so that they, and the biotic diversity they represent, will be preserved. Recreation and prettiness are secondary considerations.

In fact, I get the feeling from talking to some Nature Conservancy people that public access to the preserves is allowed not from any populist motive, but more to short-circuit charges of elitism, and to "foster local involvement."

At first I had a problem with that because I *am* a populist. I've never been able to shake the idea that the land and the game that lives on it belong to The People. When I first learned that these guys were buying up land and letting people on it to fish or whatever at the conservancy's discretion, I bristled.

But, although I may qualify as a raving radical, I'm not immune to reason. Virtually all of the land in question was privately held, and, in many cases, in more or less immediate danger of being turned into something like a shopping center or trailer park. Unless you knew the landowner or were able to slip him twenty dollars on occasion, you couldn't get on it anyway, and in the foreseeable future it would have become worthless to any sportsman and/or recreational naturalist.

And once the conservancy has it, you *can* get on most of it. A standard procedure is to allow X number of people per day. Some slots can be reserved, while others are held open for "walk-ins." There are rules. For instance, the fishing is likely to be catch-and-release with barbless flies only, and, perhaps, no hunting will be allowed, although hunting and other activities *are* allowed when it's determined that they're not detrimental to the habitat.

I thought it over and decided it was okay, although I wouldn't want all land to be like this. I think we need open land—and lots of it—where you can go on the spur of the moment, without an appointment, any day of the week the mood strikes. There are going to be times when the only answer is to go out and look at a tree or stand in a trout stream, and you can't always see those times coming two weeks in advance.

But then that's what things like national forests and wilderness areas are for. They can be crowded, especially around the easy accesses, and Ed Engle has been known to refer to an officially designated "wilderness" as a city park. Still, you can get on, and in many cases you can be alone if you'll just walk a mile or two.

Of course if you want to actually *do* anything, you have to be up on the current obscure regulations and have in your possession the proper packet of licenses and permits. It's getting complicated. Here in Colorado, for instance, the time is coming when you'll need a regular old fishing license to fish in some areas, and an extra stamp to fish in the *good* places. Naturally, I'll spring for both, even though it smacks of revenue enhancement on one hand and the smart set on the other.

The point is, the illusion—let alone the reality—of freedom is getting harder to maintain, but it can still be done.

You don't have to be a member of the conservancy to get on a preserve, any and all regular old civilians qualify and lots of people use these things. It probably won't be crowded or fished or hunted out, and it will likely be good. Habitat that supports a wide variety of species tends to be pretty luscious.

Conservancy members don't even seem to get preferential treatment, although they're the ones who know where these places are.

The people who do get preferential treatment are the potential big corporate donors with deep pockets. Steve, whose job it is to show these folks around, says the money often starts flowing as soon as people see what it's going to protect.

The money. We're not talking about raffling half a dozen trout flies for ten dollars here. We're talking about the heavy-duty stuff—six figures and up. The Nature Conservancy's ongoing Land Preservation Fund currently holds eighty-five million dollars.

There's a clean, quiet, efficient flavor to all this that sets the conservancy apart from many other conservation groups. There's no lobbying or any other kind of messy political wrangling; no army of local chapters, each with a large, volunteer board of directors with its own obscure agenda; no cumbersome banquets or functions or meetings.

The conservancy seems to be presided over by scientists,

operated by businessmen, and populated by fishermen, hunters, and bird-watchers. You could say that the makeup of the organization symbolizes the species diversity they're committed to preserving, and, like any healthy ecology, the balance comes from the tension between the different parts.

For instance, Steve once said of Phantom Canyon, "Thank God we found an endangered species in there. Now we can preserve the trout fishing." Tom Macy, a trade land specialist, is more likely to brag about the creativity and overall sweetness of the business deal that got a piece of land. One of the scientists would probably point out the general and specific reasons for preserving the biotic diversity in Phantom Canyon or anywhere else: that is, the overall health of the planet in general, and the specific possibility that something like Aletes humilis, the endangered species of wild parsley that was responsible for the Phantom Canyon purchase, could turn out to just be an unusual garnish for baked trout, or the cure for cancer or AIDS. We don't know.

Although no one in the organization has ever put it into these terms, I see their quiet, businesslike approach as a kind of counterterrorism. The enemy of the environment is big business backed by government—or, to be carefully fair about it, a certain segment of that community—and the weapon of business is money.

The Nature Conservancy is businesslike and has money. The people who actually do the deals are hardheaded, practical, and sometimes a little devious. They might be characterized as counteragents who have been lured out of the enemy camp to use what they know for a better cause. While radical groups like Earth First! dress in bear suits and stop traffic, the conservancy gets tough in a language that's understood by the bad guys. "Okay," they say, "how much do you want for it?" or maybe, "Would you care to trade it for this shopping center?"

And I mean tough. There was a piece of land in Virginia that the conservancy wanted, and it was for sale, too, but only to a developer. Seems the landowner didn't like conservation groups. So the organization—on paper and for the purpose of this deal only—became the Virginia Shores Development Company.

That disillusioned some people, and some other conservation groups have even criticized the tactic as shady. But in the language of business, let me say, shady hell, it was brilliant. It's high time we all started playing by the same rules.

If the weapon of business is money, then the delivery system is lies. They do that kind of thing to us all the time.

I've been involved in what is loosely known as the environmental community, so I know about the frustration. The group is probably species specific: into trout only or grouse only or whatever, so their outlook tends to be limited. The membership is made up of earnest folks who are good fishermen or hunters, but as conservationists they are more like foot soldiers than generals. The thing is probably run by volunteers, so even the leadership has limited time to put in, and you can't fire someone who's not doing his job because you don't employ him in the first place.

The group is relatively small, so whatever political action you take goes largely unnoticed. The group is also poor, so fundraising is a desperate enterprise, and, since the function of the club is at least partly social, you waste time and precious money on projects designed to "get the membership more involved."

To put it another way, you can end up spending all your energy on free fly-tying demonstrations and casting clinics while the rivers are being dammed. I've seen it happen.

I eventually came to a point where, if only to save my sanity, I wanted to cut the crap and see some definitive results. At the end of a long, useless meeting, that often came to me in terms of reaching for the deer rifle. The conservancy does that in more understandable and socially accepted terms. Reaching for a checkbook is the late twentieth century equivalent of saying, "Okay, you bastard, go for your gun."

If that sounds too combative, so be it. There was a time when I thought I could just be a fisherman and live a quiet little life. Now I see that, like it or not, I have to be a soldier in the trout wars.

—

We met and took turns at the last big pool. Just downstream I had stopped fishing for a few minutes to watch an osprey land in a big, dead ponderosa not thirty yards away and go about calmly eating the foot-long rainbow he'd just caught. The bird was close enough that I could tell which kind of trout he had. When I ran into Steve and A.K. I asked if they'd seen that, and they said they'd seen him *catch* it.

The top quarter of the canyon wall was still lit with sunlight, but it was dusk down on the stream, getting chilly. Dry flies were hard to see on the water, so we'd all switched to streamers.

I know from looking at the sunrise and sunset table on my small game hunting and fishing license that dusk would have fallen around 5:30 that day. If I'd been home I'd have been in front of the television watching the news, getting lulled into the assumption that the world was pretty much closed for business, and thank god for that. Things would still be horrible, and there still wouldn't be much I could do about most of it.

Down in the canyon I had no watch to consult. I don't carry one when I fish, and not to keep from getting it wet either.

A.K. and I were both fishing split bamboo rods. We do that because we like them, but also, if the truth were known, to prove some kind of obscure point. Lately I've also taken to hunting with a flintlock rifle. I think I do both not so much in the interest of trying to go back in time, but just to keep from blasting ahead with such careless speed.

The two instruments are surprisingly similar: both are still made in limited numbers for a somewhat cranky clientele, and both are old, but not what you could call outmoded. That is, they still work just fine. The bamboo fly rod catches the trout, the flintlock—when it fires—kills the rabbit whose meat goes into stew and whose fur is tied into the body of the Adams dry fly that catches the trout. And so on in a tight, neat, symbolic circle.

This is one of the things that can be forced to remain simple.

Ed says you can't be a cynic and a mystic at the same time. I say you can if you pick your examples carefully enough.

A.K. landed the last fish. It was a chunky fifteen-incher, and I took a color photo of it, even though there wasn't really enough light. That slide probably isn't salable, but I like it anyway. It shows some metallic-looking rocks, partial silhouettes of landing net and hands, and otherwise the frame is filled with a dark fish with a black, glistening eye. There's just enough bronze color to show that it's a brown trout. It's a slightly mysterious photo.

On the way back to the trail we found where something had killed and eaten a blue grouse. A coyote, maybe, though it could have been fox, bobcat, or even a mountain lion. I made a brief search for tracks or scat, Steve looked in the trees for more grouse, A.K. knelt by the remains and said, "These flank feathers make nice nymph legs."

Then we walked out of the canyon. It took an hour. On the way the conversation petered out, and I remembered a story someone had told me once about a man who'd hiked into Cardiac Canyon on the Henry's Fork and caught a fifteen-pound rainbow, by far the biggest trout of his life. Halfway back out, he threw it on the ground and left it because he couldn't carry it any farther.

It wasn't quite that bad, but it did hurt a little. Steve said that even without the limitations on access, the walk in and out would protect the place.

It was after dark when we made it up to the rim. I'd been trudging, watching my feet, and when I looked up it was all sky and stars and dizzying prairie again, almost like nothing had happened.

Way off to the west there was one single electric light, the size of a star, but yellower. When I asked Steve what it was he said, "I don't know. Maybe there's a ranch over there."

CHAPTER 18

AUTUMN

 Every fisherman has a personal set of signals that tell him fall is on the way. What I usually notice first is the color of the weeds along the trout streams. For months—long enough that it had started to feel permanent—the vegetation down by the water was the lushest and brightest green, but suddenly patches of it have begun to turn brown. This isn't a gaudy, autumn color yet, just the toasted, golden brown of wild grains going to seed in hot weather, but for me it's the first visible sign.

I'll notice this on a warm day, but I'll still get a chill up the back of my neck knowing that soon the fishing will be as good as it ever gets—a careful, low-water business with small dry flies and emergers, now and then punctuated by the razzle-dazzle of casting bright streamers to spawning browns and brookies—and then it will end. It's a mixture of excitement and poignancy, the kind of thing that can make you go sit on a rock for ten minutes to think things over.

Some people like to picture the seasons in such rigid increments that you can actually place the first moment of fall at the autumnal equinox on September 23 or 24, but it's much sneakier than that. Fishermen know that autumn isn't really a season at all, just a time of year when the seasons *change*.

First the stream flows drop, or, more properly, you notice one day that they *have* dropped. The stream seems smaller, the rocks seem bigger, and the high-water stain has drifted farther up the bank. Things begin to look exposed to the weather and you get an uneasy feeling, as though you'd left something out overnight that should have been brought in, but you can't remember what.

There are still grasshoppers in those dry weeds, but not as many of them as before, and the trout aren't as easily convinced as before either. Oh sure, they still like hoppers, in fact they're fat from eating them, but suddenly the fish are skeptical of the big, bushy, summer patterns. This is when I root through the box looking for some of those low-water hoppers, the kind with the thinner bodies, lower wings, and sparse legs. Some years I discover that I never got around to tying them back in February when the snows were getting wet and springlike and May or June was as far into the future as I cared to look.

Not looking far enough ahead. It might occur to me that there's probably an appropriate quote on this somewhere in Shakespeare, but a feeling of mild desperation has descended and there doesn't seem to be time to go thumbing through books. That's winter stuff and will come soon enough as it is.

I think the streams are especially pretty in the fall. With less water in them, they're slower, almost lazy, and brilliantly clear, with virtually every grain of sediment settled out of them. You can spot the trout much more easily now—almost as easily as they can spot you. They don't like exposing themselves to feed in the clear, shallow water, but they do it because the bugs are there and the fish are hungry.

Fishing lore says the trout "know" that winter is coming and things will be getting very tough soon, so they stock up, putting on fat like bears. Well, maybe they know and maybe they don't, but their psychology does seem to change. They're eager to feed, but they're also jumpy and cautious. They seem nervous and impatient, or at least that's how we feel when we act that way, and so we anthropomorphize, putting that on the trout so we can understand them better and, presumably, catch a few of them. They may seem relaxed and casual, but try getting too close, or making a sloppy cast, or wading too loudly, or throwing your shadow on the water, or even just dragging your fly a little.

Every fall I'm reminded just how fast a trout can move.

On some of the streams I fish regularly, I find myself switching from the standard summer casting position to the autumn one; the pool I used to cast to from there I now have to work from way back here. This creates the illusion that things are getting smaller and farther away. It's a longer cast and a trickier drift, but it becomes necessary. On smaller streams I'm down on my knees to keep my silhouette lower.

Some spots are best fished from the opposite direction in the fall. Many places where I could make a smart upstream cast in the summer are now slower and smoother flowing with less chop to cover the cast. The pools are more alert and need a long, surgical downstream drift.

By October of most years, I'm wading more slowly to keep the surface ripples and overall commotion down, making longer, more gentle casts, and have developed the fall fly fisher's skulking crouch. Some seasons I have to force myself into the thoughtful, stealthy approach, while in others it just seems to happen by itself. Either way, by the time it's turning cool enough that I'm regularly carrying a wool sweater and hat in the back pouch of the vest, I've convinced myself that I am one crafty fisherperson. The hat and sweater are dark in the interest of camouflage.

My leaders have grown longer, too, and the tippets are lighter. As a rule of thumb, I fish a 4 or 5x tippet because I've decided that's limp enough for a good drift in most spots, but still strong enough to let me play a decent-sized trout with some authority. In the summer I can get away with the 4x more often than some of my dry fly fishing friends would like to think is possible, but as autumn wears on I'm down to 6 or 7x—and some of the guys seem to feel much better about that.

I'm not convinced that trout actually see a heavier leader and spook as some fishermen claim. I believe they either don't see the leader at all, or that they see it just fine, but don't care about it one way or the other. What they *do* care about is how natural the drift of the fly is. Your trout fly should be helplessly bobbing along on every crease and ripple because that's what the real bugs around it are doing and fish pay close attention to these things, having very little else to do with their time. In the clear, slow currents of autumn, a few thousanths of an inch more or less in the monofilament department can make a noticeable difference. All of a sudden a dry fly tied to a 4x leader can drift as if it's wired to a stick.

By now—late September, maybe October—the distinctive fall hatches have begun to show up. Around here it's the Blue-winged Olive mayfly, the small, pale Baetis in size 18 or 20, sometimes mixed with, or followed by, the *Little* Blue-winged Olive, a different insect with a five-syllable name that is just the same fly in a size 22 or 24, unless you want to go out of your way to impress someone with the Latin.

These bugs seem to be designed especially for the season. They're a grayish olive color with a hint of chilly blue, not unlike the overcast skies they like to hatch under. They're small, but not fragile-looking like some mayflies. Instead they give the impression of being tough and wiry. You're not surprised to see them hatching in regulation duck weather.

The patterns used amount to a kind of seasonal progression. At first, the over-the-counter hackled, dubbed, Blue-winged Olive dry fly will work well, especially when the water is a little on the swift side, although I now prefer the trimmer Olive Dun Quill as tied by A.K. That fly is catching on now and they sell by the hundreds of dozens around here in the fall. That's good for A.K., who makes his living as a flytier, but I kind of miss those first few seasons when I'd bummed some dyed quills from him, copied his prototypes, and it was our little secret.

Autumn can make you sentimental about a once-secret fly becoming popular, and also about things changing in general. It was in the fall one year when my ex-girlfriend, Deirdre, asked me, "Are your friends older than mine or just more beat up?" and I had to admit, "Uh, a little of both, I guess."

That's the sort of thing that can pass unnoticed in July, but in October it can make me consider taking a long, slow, solitary walk downtown, maybe to find a dingy little bar with some quiet jazz on the jukebox. Not to get depressed, but just to mull things over.

Perhaps I run into my lawyer on the way, out on the cold street in nothing but his suit coat, hurrying. He's on his way to sue someone, to, as he puts it, "Drill this guy a new anus."

"Do you ever feel bad about that?" I ask.

"Never," he says. "In this capacity I am simply the Instrument of Karma."

Lawyers are like nuclear weapons. By all rights they shouldn't exist, but if some people have them, then you'd better have one, too, just in case. I could find a nicer lawyer, but not a better one.

It strikes me that this is how grown-ups think. I remember my father getting mad at me when I was nineteen, saying things like, "You won't be so goddamned radical once you see how things really are," and, "Wait till you have a family and responsibilities of your own. Then you won't be so foolhardy."

Those sounded like threats, but I think now they were offered as honest bits of advice in the only tone of voice he had left for me. Bad advice, maybe, but heartfelt. Dad thought like a grown-up. I try not to, although there are days when it's unavoidable.

This is what autumn can do to you if you stay in town wasting time trying to sort things out. I might think, it's one thing to be forty-two and still wondering who you are; at least you haven't started worrying about who you should have been.

But I don't stay in town because there are trout to be caught. I honestly don't know why I fish. Or, rather, I fish in order to save my life; I just don't know *why* it saves my life. Maybe it's nothing more mysterious than the engrossing questions that come up.

For instance, what do you do when the trout seem to have figured it all out and the Olive Dun Quills and Blue-winged Olives start drawing short strikes and refusals? (With the usual fly-fisher's paranoia, I prefer the former pattern, but carry both, just in case.)

I usually go to the no-hackle with hen tip wings then, while others like the thorax tie or the Iwamasa dun, and still others use all kinds of contraptions with things like burned wings and extended bodies that are harder to tie but also more "accurate." Everyone has a Plan B, and because flotation is less crucial in the lower, smoother currents, some of them can get pretty exotic.

That's if you want to stay with the proper dry fly. Sometimes the fish will go off the winged flies entirely and get selective to the emergers and floating nymphs. There are all kinds of patterns for that, too, several of which I carry. Now that I think about it, I have more different fly patterns for this one hatch than any other I've ever fished. I use them all in a season, sometimes several in a single day.

I might fish a Beatis nymph deep in the hour before the hatch starts when the nymphs are beginning to move and the trout are just picking up on them; then switch to the emerger or floating nymph as the hatch builds up; then go to a winged dry fly late in the emergence when there are no more nymphs left and the trout are sniffing out the last of the duns.

And then maybe I'll try a little spent-wing dry on those sporadic, late risers that are taking the crippled duns in the backwaters and eddies. So far I've stopped short of wiggle nymphs and stillborn duns, more because there's no room left in the box than because I've actually ruled them out.

It's painstaking. The fly has to be either right or damned close, the drift usually has to be the same, the leader should be fine, and the cast must be made from far enough away that the fish aren't spooked. And it's not just that hatch—lots of fall dry-fly fishing goes the same way.

Some days the good old dead drift float doesn't even work. Those are the times when some of the natural flies are hopping on the surface trying to get airborne and the trout are too cagey to eat a fly, no matter how pretty it is, that isn't hopping with the rest of them. Trout can be real bastards sometimes.

So you have to put that subtle twitch on your fly just as it enters the field of vision of the fish in question. Not too soon, not too late, and not six inches to one side or the other. This

takes better timing, a more accurate cast, finer line control and
a tighter grip on your nerves.

You feel pretty good when it works and, interestingly enough,
it works often because you're at the end of a season's worth of
practice when you're about as hot as you're going to get. And for
some reason you're catching these fish as if something rather
important depended on it.

The fall hatches tend to start earlier in the shorter days, more
like afternoon than evening, and as they progress I'm *wearing* the
wool sweater and hat instead of packing them. Now the cargo
pouch in the vest has a rain slicker in it. This is something I hope
I'll have to use because the gloomiest days are usually the best,
and a drizzling rain is perfect. The bugs like to hatch in a low
light and the cold and damp keep their wings from drying too
quickly, so they're on the water longer.

Things seem to be caught in a kind of tension. The bugs are
slow and a little dopey from the cold, the trout are quick and
efficient, and the humans fish with a bit more determination
than usual.

Nasty weather can wear thin after a while, but at first it's
pleasant after the hot summer: invigorating. Those bright, crisp
fall days are real pretty, but the hatches are usually thinner and
the fish are tougher. Trout get smart in the fall. On heavily
fished streams, they have the same season behind them that you
have and, although they're not as smart as we sometimes make
them out to be, they're not exactly stupid, either.

And boy, are they handsome. A fall trout is at the end of a
good long summer growing season. In most streams he's as well
fed, fat and healthy as he's going to get this year, and he seems
to know it. A big, fall trout always looks to me like he's proud of
himself for having done so well—and also a little embarrassed at
having been caught.

Rainbows and cutthroats have gotten chubby and they fight
with as much weight as speed. Even the smaller fish throb in the
fall, where in the summer they just wiggled. The browns and
brookies, as they ease into their spawning colors, are unsur-
passed. Their earth-colored browns, yellows, and olives are deep

and moist, and their hot oranges are electric. Yes, those are the same colors the surrounding countryside is going into. That can't just be a coincidence, can it?

New England falls are famous for their colors. The Midwest I remember from my childhood wasn't half bad either. Out here in the Rocky Mountains, it's a little more sedate for the most part. The willows and cottonwoods on the plains turn yellow, then brown. In the high country, stands of aspen do about the same, sometimes with a little fringe of orange around the edges, and people drive up there on October weekends to see them.

But the real autumn out here happens along the trout streams. Whether they flow through sagebrush plains, deciduous groves, or pine and spruce forests, there's always a ribbon of leafy bushes on the banks—things like staghorn sumac, dogwood, and others whose names I don't know—that fill in the otherwise missing shades of red. Up in the spruce forests, the autumn changes are often just shoulder high and only a few yards wide. The rest of the woods are the same green they always are, giving the mountains that well-advertised timeless feeling. On the right kind of day, it can be enough to break your heart.

The fall hatches usually work their way down from the higher altitudes, so that brookies and cutts in the little mountain streams may be eating Blue-winged Olives while the browns lower down are still looking at Red Quills and maybe even some Ginger Quills. If a Blue-winged Olive is the color of a drizzly sky, a Red Quill is like dogwood bark, and the Ginger Quill is like a turning cottonwood—those scientifically formulated color charts notwithstanding.

The spawning runs work their way downhill, too, starting early up high and later down low. Supposedly the itch to spawn in trout is triggered by a combination of the length of the days and the temperature of the water. Although the days are the same, the water cools sooner at the higher altitudes, so I have come to believe that water temperature is the deciding factor.

Early can be *real* early. I've seen brook trout running up feeder creeks from mountain lakes in late August and, on the

same drainage, fished for spawning browns under bare cottonwoods after Thanksgiving.

Some fishermen around here actively chase the spawning runs
for the big trout. There's enough water, and enough changes in
elevation, that you can do this with some hope of success for up
to three months in a good year. For most of us, though, it's more
haphazard than that. We just fish the hatches. In the fall, we fish
almost daily if we can, though we're never far from the
knowledge that bigger trout than most of the ones we've seen all
season are, at this very moment, starting to get a little randy. It's
like an extra tingling in the air. I think there's much power
generated by a population of creatures that get horny only once
a year, all at the same time. We humans with our year-around
mating season can't really relate to that, but I think we're still
connected enough to scent it on the breeze.

So we just fish, and sure enough, we now and then stumble
upon pods of browns or brookies noodling and chasing each
other around in the gravelly shallows.

Okay, we do hunt them up to some extent. For instance, if the
dry fly fishing is a bit slow on a brook trout pond, it's not long
before someone has beached his float tube and is prancing up
the inlet stream through yellow willows and red dogwoods,
stalking the riffles. You know he's found spawners when he stops
to re-rig his leader and change flies.

By the way, when I say "we," I mean the fishermen who love
big trout as much as anyone but who are still hesitant to put away
our dry flies. And you do have to put away the dries and fish
streamers when you're after spawners, unless, of course, you're
some kind of raving purist. You can, in fact, move a spawning
brown to a dry fly if you try long and hard—I've seen it done—
but it proves a point that's too obscure for my taste.

The accepted fly is the streamer and the accepted theory is,
the spawning trout sees the streamer as competition (in the case
of the male), a bait fish or young trout trying to steal eggs (in the
case of the hen fish), or as an all-around pain in the ass for both.
It's not food as it would be at other times of the year.

If fall dry fly fishing is a matter of subtle trickery, of convincing the feeding trout that nothing whatsoever is the least bit out of the ordinary, then casting a streamer to a spawning trout is the exact opposite; it's a deliberate disturbance, an intrusion designed to make the fish mad.

I like to get upstream from the fish I've picked out—far enough up that he can't see me, close enough that I can see him—and swing the streamer fly right past his nose. On the rare occasions when the fish is already in a raspy mood, he'll hit it instinctively on the first cast. More likely he'll flare at it, or glance at it impatiently, and let it go by.

It can take quite a few casts before he'll follow it, and even then he may not actually bite it. Remember, he doesn't want to eat the thing, he just wants it to go away. If he thinks he's chased it off, he's satisfied. It sometimes helps to stop the streamer when the fish charges at it. It's not running like it should, the trout is seriously fed up by now, so he nips at it, and you've got him.

He'll be heavy and bright and a little wild-eyed. He's also likely to be pretty big. Holding him in the net, you think, Where the hell have you been all summer?

My main streamer for this is a simple bucktail with lots of orange in it; saltwater grade fluorescent orange, the kind you can pick out at twenty yards in low light. This color is the spawning flag for both brookies and browns and I think it trips some kind of territorial switch in the big males.

Naturally, it doesn't always work, in which case I try a black Wooly Bugger. No theory here, it's just a good fly, and also a different one—something to switch to when theory runs into reality and reality won't give.

Catching trout while they're busy spawning can sometimes feel a little unfair—"How would *you* like it?" is the standard comment from those who disapprove. I guess I'm still ambivalent on the issue. I do it where it's legal (as it is more often than not) because, well, there are the trout; big, bright ones on display in the clear, shallow riffle, and here I am with a fly rod and a dozen orange bucktails in my pocket. I've always been weak in the face of temptation and, frankly, trout are the least of my worries in that regard.

Then, too, it's ominously close to the end of the year, November maybe, cold, dismal, late. Half the fishermen you know are out hunting deer or already have one in the freezer. It may be that you actually deserve this last big trout, even though catching it isn't the kindest thing you can think of under the circumstances. Maybe once the stream is frozen over and covered with snow you'll stop to consider where kindness fits in all this.

I can usually satisfy myself by trying to catch the biggest spawner I can locate (or the biggest two or three) and then quitting. I'm not a bleeding heart, but I have some sympathy.

But not quitting entirely, of course. As I said, there's lots of water around here, so if the spawning fish are brookies, there are probably some cutthroats in the neighborhood that are still just feeding and are, therefore, fair game. If the spawners are browns, there may be some rainbows around. Sometimes the bows will lie downstream from the browns to pick off stray eggs, and you can take them on miniature orange egg flies. Also fair game, if not entirely classy in some nymph fishing circles.

Some years, if the weather holds off long enough, there's even some dry fly fishing to post-spawning browns or brook trout as they rise—lazily now, seemingly more out of habit than real hunger—to hatches of midges, the last and smallest of the bugs.

These are the days of size 26 emergers, 8x tippets, frozen fingers, and lonely trout streams with snowy banks. Ice forms in the line guides, and when you take the lunch break you may feel the need for a small bankside fire. The spawners have lost much of their color, as if it dissolved in the stinging cold water the same way your fingers now go white and numb when you handle a fish.

Now that it's all but over, you're suddenly stalking like a bobcat, casting beautifully, and playing fish with what you can't help but see as great artistry. Put away the modesty and face it, you have gotten pretty damned good at this. The first good snowstorm caught you on the stream, and you felt good about that, but you're still bundling up and slipping in days on the water, not quite willing to pack it in for the year.

Before the parka and wool millar mitt weather arrived, you saw fall as an appropriate finale. The fishing was great and *you* were great, like you were made for each other. It was the kind of thing that gives hope for your own ongoing future with the suggestion that things can mature nicely and be better toward the end than they were in the beginning. It was a nice idea when the mayflies were still on, but now the leaves are all down and if you didn't know better you'd swear it was March. You're forced to admit it: the trout are few and far between and you're freezing your poor little ass off.

It's still pretty out there—in a spare, wintry sort of way—but the urgency has faded some and you're beginning to get pensive. You're wondering what it's supposed to mean; what you're supposed to do with the skills and patience you've learned over the last season, and the accumulated seasons before that—"over the years," in fact, though you might avoid thinking in terms of passing years at a moment like this.

Well, if nothing else, you can enjoy the view.